Praise for *Found in Transition*

"In this engrossing and sometimes heart-wrenching account, pediatrician Hassouri describes Ava's...transition from male to female with approachable, empathetic language that bridges gaps in understanding about the transition process. The author's unflinching honesty about her initial ignorance regarding trans issues is refreshing, and her unwavering adherence to truth makes the story both compelling and edifying....A moving and relatable story of love and heartache...a unique parenting story that has plenty to say about families in general."

— *Kirkus Reviews*

"I really can't imagine a better book not only to help parents going through similar struggles but also, truly, to help us all rethink the expectations we impose on our kids from the day they are born. Paria Hassouri, blindsided and fearful at first, shows us what it looks like to find acceptance and grace, and how transformative and uplifting that awakening can be if we are open to it."

— **Hilary Liftin,** author of *Movie Star by Lizzie Pepper*

"In this open, honest, and relatable memoir, Paria Hassouri invites the reader on a journey through the initial resistance and eventual embrace of her child's gender transition. *Found in Transition* speaks to the power of parental love and trusting our children to grow into the people they know themselves to be."

— **Abigail C. Saguy,** UCLA professor of sociology and author of *Come Out, Come Out, Whoever You Are*

"A beautiful, honest, utterly engaging story of a mother's love. It will inspire your heart and stay with you for a long time."

— **Tembi Locke,** *New York Times* bestselling author of *From Scratch*

"*Found in Transition* is a narrative of hope for anyone who has ever navigated identity. Paria Hassouri lays bare her own struggles, ultimately demonstrating the idea of *family* as a verb, proving that such stories are vital to this cultural moment, and that love indeed endures."

— **Shawna Kenney,** author and writing instructor,
UCLA Extension Writers Program

"*Found in Transition* is simply beautiful — heart-opening and mind-expanding. Paria Hassouri invites us on her journey from resistance to acceptance of her daughter Ava's trans identity, and in doing so reminds us that spiritual growth takes commitment and work, and that to love and accept one another as we are is the greatest gift we can give."

— **Scott Stabile,** author of
Big Love: The Power of Living with a Wide-Open Heart

"A brave, bare, humble, and honest portrayal of a mother coming to understand her child's experience. This much-needed book gives voice to the common journey of bewildered parents trying to do right by their child, especially those supporting adolescents with gender dysphoria — disbelief, anxiety, protectiveness, uncertainty, and love, love, love. *Found in Transition* is also a great resource for medical professionals to help them understand the real experiences of families with transgender teens."

— **Amy Weimer, MD,** medical director,
UCLA Gender Health Program

FOUND
in
TRANSITION

FOUND
in
TRANSITION

A MOTHER'S EVOLUTION DURING
HER CHILD'S GENDER CHANGE

Paria Hassouri, MD

New World Library
Novato, California

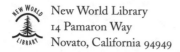

New World Library
14 Pamaron Way
Novato, California 94949

Text design by Tona Pearce Myers

Library of Congress Cataloging-in-Publication Data

Names: Hassouri, Paria, date, author.
Title: Found in transition : a mother's evolution during her child's gender change / Paria Hassouri, MD.
Description: Novato, California : New World Library, [2020] | Summary: "In this autobiographical narrative, an Iranian-American pediatrician and mother of three is blindsided when one of her children comes out as transgender. As the author grapples with her child's transition from male to female, she is forced to reexamine her ideas of parenting, gender, and personal identity."-- Provided by publisher.
Identifiers: LCCN 2020022089 (print) | LCCN 2020022090 (ebook) | ISBN 9781608687084 (hardback) | ISBN 9781608687091 (Ebook)
Subjects: LCSH: Hassouri, Paria, date | Transgender children. | Parents of sexual minority youth. | Identity (Psychology) | Gender-nonconforming children.
Classification: LCC HQ77.9 .H37 2020 (print) | LCC HQ77.9 (ebook) | DDC 306.874/3092 [B]--dc23
LC record available at https://lccn.loc.gov/2020022089
LC ebook record available at https://lccn.loc.gov/2020022090

First printing, September 2020
ISBN 978-1-60868-708-4
Ebook ISBN 978-1-60868-709-1
Printed in the United States on 30% postconsumer-waste recycled paper

 New World Library is proud to be a Gold Certified Environmentally Responsible Publisher. Publisher certification awarded by Green Press Initiative.

10 9 8 7 6 5 4 3 2 1

For Ava, who always teaches me much more than I can ever hope to teach her, and every other child brave enough to live their truth.

And for every parent struggling with making the best decisions for their child with the knowledge that they have.

Minds are like parachutes: they only function when open.

— Thomas Robert Dewar

CONTENTS

THANKSGIVING 2017: IRON

"Mom, I left something on my bed for you to iron," my fourteen-year-old says when he sees me come downstairs. The hair on the back of my neck rises, my heart starts galloping in my chest, but I reply with the most casual, nonchalant "Okay" I can muster.

It is Thanksgiving Day. We are going to leave for my mom's in just a couple of hours. I hate ironing. I avoid buying clothes that are difficult to iron, and when my husband occasionally asks me to iron something for him while he jumps in the shower, I get irritated every time. Yet within half an hour of my son's request, I find myself back upstairs and ironing his dress without saying a word, while trying to calm the panicky thoughts in my head. Never in any of my visions of myself as a mother had I imagined a scene like this, yet here I am.

We are waiting for an appointment with my child's third therapist in six months, which have probably been the hardest six months of my life. It's been difficult to shut down my racing mind for even one minute. "I wish," "I want," "I fear," and "What if" statements have taken over my brain and will not give it a moment of respite. As the iron goes back and forth over the maroon H&M dress my son must have bought at the mall on his own, I find myself in a trance, praying to a God that my agnostic

self has never really believed in. I am bargaining and pleading and nego-
tiating with the universe:

Dear God or Universe, if this is true, if he is a girl, why weren't there
any signs? Why didn't he ever want to be a princess or play with dolls or
grow his hair or show an interest in baking or give any single sign that he
might be a girl?

Dear Universe, please let him be safe. What if he gets beaten up or bul-
lied? What if he hurts himself? Please let no one hurt him. Please let me not
be scared every time I get a phone call from a number I don't recognize.

Dear God, what if he really is a trans girl? When and how do I say
goodbye to the child I thought I knew and accept the new one? If he isn't a
girl and this is just some teenage angst he is going through, how unhappy
and depressed and lost must he be to believe that changing his gender is the
answer? What kind of parent have I been to raise a child who is this lost?
How can I say that I'm his mother, when I don't know him? All I've ever
wanted is to be a mother, and now I'm questioning my own identity as one.

Dear God, how am I going to send him to college? Who will his college
roommates be? He can't be in a room with boy roommates; he will feel so out
of place. He can't room with girls; they may not be comfortable with him.
He can't be in a single dorm room or apartment, even more isolated than he
already is, at even higher risk for hurting himself. He can't live at home. He
can't, I can't. I need him out and independent and not in my face all the time.
But how will I sleep when he isn't under my roof where I can check on him?

Dear God, if this is true, please let this not be the first thing people no-
tice about him. My baby is brilliant and has the biggest heart in the world.
Please let people see that when they see him. Please don't let them see a trans
girl before they see the brilliance of his mind or the size of his heart.

Dear God or Universe, if he is a trans girl, then please let me see him as
a girl one day, not just call him by a new name and refer to him as her. If he
really is a girl, please let me one day look at him and see my daughter, see her
in my heart as who she is, not as the boy that I carried and nursed and raised
and lost, but just as my beautiful daughter. Please. Please.

I don't remember if I first told my husband that Aydin had asked me to iron his outfit for today and it was a dress, or if I first texted my sister, who was already at my mom's house, so she could warn my mother that Aydin would be coming in a dress. I just remember that after ironing it, I laid it back on his bed, my hands shaking, and told them both.

For the remainder of this book, I refer to my middle child as my daughter Ava, and I use the female pronouns *she* and *her*, even when I am talking about her past, before I came to accept and see her as a girl. It may take a few pages to adjust to this use of *she* and *her* when I am describing a time in my journey when I still clearly saw her as my son; however, knowing what I know today, I use female pronouns even in reference to her past, to honor the girl she was on the inside even before she knew it herself. I also often use her current legal name, Ava, to refer to her even at times before we used it. This is to minimize the use of her birth name, Aydin, which the trans community often refers to as one's "dead" name. I use male pronouns and her old name only when I directly quote conversations, correspondence, or my own thoughts from the past.

I'M *a* GIRL

My cell phone rang. It was May 24, 2017, and although it was only 5 a.m. Thailand time, my husband and I were not in bed. Babak and I had just left our little bungalow on Ko Phangan to head to the beach. We had decided the night before to set an alarm so that we could catch the magical sunrise at least one morning while we were there. Being at the Sanctuary on Ko Phangan was like being on Gilligan's Island. We had flown from Los Angeles to Taipei, Taipei to Bangkok, and Bangkok to Ko Samui, and then finally taken a little boat from the island of Ko Samui to the smaller island of Ko Phangan. For this yoga retreat, we had definitely broken our rule of "we won't go anywhere we can't fly direct."

Babak was relatively new to yoga, so the trip was not his idea. I'd been following the instructor, Jake, for at least five years, but I wouldn't exactly describe myself as a yogi, either. I had stumbled into one of Jake's classes. It wasn't the yoga, but his words that brought me repeatedly back to his classes, often finding myself in tears during savasana, lying still at the end of class. Jake shared anecdotes about his childhood or about self-doubt, about using yoga in the continual process of self-healing. His words took me back to being in middle school. I was one of only a handful of brown kids in a suburb of Pittsburgh, Pennsylvania, desperately wanting to not be different, to belong. On the mat at the end of Jake's classes, I came to realize that a part of me was still that little girl, trying to prove my worth despite all my accomplishments and looking for acceptance. I started "stalking" Jake, seeking the rare occasion when his class time didn't conflict with my hectic schedule. One day, I wrote what his class meant to me in a blog post and then printed the post and handed it to him in an envelope at the end of class. I was afraid that once he read my words, he'd think I was crazy, but I took the chance. I had to show him that his words mattered, that sharing these personal details with his students mattered.

That was the beginning of our friendship. Eventually, I made a whole group of yoga friends, who subsequently became friends with Babak, and several of us went on the ten-day retreat together, without our kids. I knew that all that travel and all those connections would be worth the magical experience Jake would provide. And it had been magical, up until that phone call.

We had left our busy lives as two physicians living and practicing in the heart of Beverly Hills and landed on a tropical island with no cars and no television. When I asked the Sanctuary's barista if there was any way to get a coffee before our first morning yoga session, he replied, amused, "No. Why do you need coffee earlier than eight? You're on vacation." I soon learned that I could flow from warrior two to half moon pose without a drop of caffeine. I also gave up any attempt to put on makeup: it would just melt on my face in the humidity. I put my hair in a ponytail, exposing my true "I woke up like this" face, and even stopped shaving my legs because there were too many mosquito bites to work around. All the clothes I'd packed had been unnecessary; the air was too sticky to wear anything other than a sports bra and shorts or a bathing suit.

Hairstyling, makeup, and clothes — the security blankets of my adulthood, which helped compensate for what I felt I lacked in my teen years — had no place on the island. Even my running clothes and shoes did not leave the suitcase, since the longest beach on the island was only about a quarter of a mile. The new identity I had worked so hard to establish over the last five years, that of runner, had nowhere to roam on Ko Phangan. But the three daily yoga sessions, interspersed with swimming in the Gulf of Thailand, in a place free from smog and a single honking car horn, let alone a symphony of them, was exactly what I'd needed. The only symphonies were the sounds of the tropics, and the food — vegan Thai food that didn't need fake cashew cheese or curry sauce to make it not just palatable but mouthwatering.

My parents were staying with our three kids back in Los Angeles. School was still in session, and our kids were in tenth, eighth, and fifth grade. We would make it back just in time for fifth- and eighth-grade "graduation." My mother, who had always been chronically late picking me up from school, leaving me waiting on the front bench alone and wanting to crawl out of my own skin, had assured me she would get all three kids back and forth to school and all their activities on time. It had been a long time since Babak and I had been on a vacation alone together, and our eighteenth anniversary coincided with the retreat dates, so the timing seemed right.

My phone rang, and the screen showed a Los Angeles number I didn't recognize. It was Mr. Wilson, the vice principal of the middle school. "We know you're in Thailand and it is still very early there. We waited as late as we could in the school day before calling you. Everything is okay, but we still had to call." If I was going to get a call from school, of course it would be about my middle child. The calls had started in kindergarten, and they were *always* about my middle child.

The history teacher, Ms. Lewis, was on the line with Mr. Wilson, and she took over. "Aydin told me that he is hurting himself because he has something he hasn't told you, and he doesn't know how to tell you."

Suddenly I couldn't breathe. Never before had Aydin — whom we now call Ava — tried in any way to hurt herself. The other phone calls from school had always been about her being depressed or getting upset in class. Even a teacher who ignored her raised hand, wanting to give other kids the chance to answer a question once in a while, could upset her enough to require the school counselor to intervene. But the phone calls had never been about physical harm. And when we left Los Angeles, Ava seemed happier than she had been in years. She had just finished playing the Pirate King in the school's production of *The Pirates of Penzance*, and as I watched her sing "Oh Better Far to Live and Die" in a deep baritone voice, waving her sword and stomping her booted feet, I thought to myself, *I've never seen him happier. I'm so happy that he's finally found himself.*

Mr. Wilson said, "He has been using scissors to try to cut his wrists." I couldn't believe it. Ava was always scared of everything, so cautious even when using a butter knife. They had to be mistaken. The history teacher continued, "He told us that he is questioning his gender identity, and he thinks he is a girl. He didn't know how to tell you, and the thought of telling you caused him enough distress to try to hurt himself."

My head started spinning. "This doesn't sound right. This doesn't sound like my child. He is not a girl. He has never done anything that would suggest that he has any gender identity issues. We talk all the time. We've talked a lot in the last year."

Ms. Lewis said, "I think there is probably something to what he is saying. We talked for a long time. You have an amazing child. He was very worried about me sharing our conversation with you."

It didn't seem believable that Ava would be scared to talk to me, given all the conversations we routinely had, let alone hurt herself over it. "Look, he told his dad and me in the fall that he is bisexual. I think he is gay. He put on eyeliner for the school musical, and he really liked it. He doesn't realize that you can be a gay boy and wear eyeliner or makeup for fun sometimes."

The morning after the first performance of *Pirates of Penzance*, Ava had come down to the kitchen. "Mom, I did try washing my face, but I couldn't get all the eyeliner off, so I'm just going to go to school like this."

I looked at her eyes, the previous night's eyeliner still mostly visible. "That's fine," I had replied. A few days later I found her phone filled with selfies that were zoomed in on her lined eyes and thought, *Yup, he's gay.*

"Believe me, I know my child," I rambled defensively to Ms. Lewis. "I'm going to sort this all out when I get back." But she repeated that based on their conversation, she thought that it was possible Ava really was experiencing gender dysphoria (distress over sex and gender assigned at birth). I kept talking back, defending, disputing. *Who does she think she is?* I thought. *She had one conversation with my child, and thinks she knows him better than I do?*

We were on the phone for at least an hour while I paced back and forth on the beach. Babak kept trying to ask me what was going on, and I mouthed to him, "It's the school. It's Aydin, again." Mr. Wilson said they hadn't told my parents why Ava had tried to hurt herself, only what she had done, and I felt myself breathe a sigh of relief. The last thing I needed was my mom trying to address this with my child and saying the wrong things, or criticizing me as a mother for raising an utterly confused child.

At some point, the sun rose, but I didn't notice it. I kept arguing, defending, denying, reassuring, while Babak sat on the beach staring at the horizon. I never asked him if he actually noticed the sunrise or just sat there and wondered what was happening on the other end of that line.

Once I hung up, we walked back to our little bungalow, and I told him about the conversation. We both cried. I wept not because I thought Ava might be trans, which I didn't consider even a remote possibility, but because she had tried to hurt herself, because she was so lost and confused, or depressed, or attention seeking, or whatever she was that made her resort to self-harm. I cried because I was tired of being her mother.

We called my mom. Ava had been the one who insisted the school not tell her grandparents the reason she was harming herself. My mom tried to reassure us that everything was fine. They had picked Ava up from school and talked to her, and although they didn't know why she had done it, she really seemed fine. We were not due to fly back for another five days, but we said we'd look into getting home earlier.

"No, you don't need to do that," my mom said. "Raising teenagers is hard. These things are going to keep coming up. You guys need a little time together and to invest in each other if you are going to get through these next years with your kids. We're here. We're watching him."

We then spoke to Ava herself. She was crying. I could picture her, phone to her ear, head and shoulders slumped, trying to disappear. "Listen, I love you. Everything is going to be okay," I tried to reassure her.

"Did the school tell you why?" she asked, her voice barely audible.

"Yes, they did," I answered, although I didn't spell out "The school said you think you are a girl." I couldn't say the words. "Don't worry about the why. We'll talk about all of that when we get home. We'll figure this out. We love you. There is nothing worth hurting yourself over. I need you to promise to never do that again. We love you. Everything is going to be okay."

"But they told you the reason?" she asked again. Maybe she wasn't sure I really understood. She probably needed to hear me say the words "You believe you are a girl, and that's okay," but I didn't say them. I wouldn't say them. This was the first of many times that I would fail her over the next few months.

"Yes, they told us. Don't worry about the why," I said again. "We can figure this all out when we get back. We love you." My words probably sounded to her like "We'll fix this, this part of you that is broken and needs to be fixed."

Then she spoke to her dad, her Baba. I heard mutterings of love and "It's going to be okay." When he hung up, we sat there crying, unsure of what to do. We couldn't just hop on the next flight home. This is what happens when you break your rule of "we won't fly anywhere we can't go direct" in the biggest possible way. We decided to go to our 8 a.m. yoga session and come back and see what flights we could arrange, then deal with getting a private boat to take us off Ko Phangan.

To get to our yoga class, we walked through the jungle and up the equivalent of seven or eight flights of stairs made up of mud, dirt, and wooden planks to a platform with a straw roof and mosquito-netting walls. The steep climb up each time was meditative and left me breathless.

Just when I thought I couldn't handle more steps, I reached the yoga hut. The space was magical, suspended in the middle of a jungle.

But as we walked up this time, my mind was racing rather than calm. We rolled out our mats, hearts heavy, teary-eyed. Usually, we arrived for class early to warm up a little. On that day, we were the last to get there. We looked around at the group. Babak was the one to tell them we'd gotten some bad news about one of our kids from home and might have to leave the retreat early. He knew that if I opened my mouth, choking sobs would pour out instead of words. The tears started to stream down my face, and I just nodded to Jake to start class so I could close my eyes and start breathing. I needed to breathe.

About half the group were good friends we'd known before going on the retreat; the other half were acquaintances or people we'd met there. We told our friends everything. One of the many blessings we've had is friends that we could tell everything to from the start — friends who made no judgments, who kept things confidential, who held our hands and lent us their ears and wiped away our tears as often as we needed. Later, when I talked to other families going through the same thing, I learned that many of them had had to keep everything to themselves, many had friends and family who didn't understand, and many coupled parents were at odds with one another. We never had to worry about judgment or lack of understanding from friends. For me, someone who can't hold anything in, whose eyes betray me even before the words spill out, our friends' compassion was sanity saving.

After class, we went back to our bungalow and started making phone calls. The best travel arrangements we could make would get us home only two days earlier, at a significant cost. We didn't know what to do. On the one hand, my mom kept reassuring us that everything was fine and urging us to take this time to be together. On the other hand, Babak kept reiterating, "I can't imagine that our child is going through something like this and we are halfway around the world while it's happening."

We ended up staying, but I later found out just how much the intervening days had shaken up my parents. My mom had given us all those reassurances because she knew it would be hard for us to change our plans, but until we got back, she was on constant guard. She kept finding reasons to go into Ava's room to check on her, or send her older brother, Armon, in to see what she was doing. She got up multiple times in the night to check and make sure Ava was in her bed and sleeping. When we got back, she finally confessed, "I don't think I can stay with them again for a long time. I can't be responsible for watching teenagers, and you shouldn't travel anywhere far." She couldn't handle the possibility of something happening while they were in her care. I had already decided we wouldn't be taking any more trips until all three kids were in college. One of us would always stay with them if the other had to travel, and any parent getaways would be limited to one weekend a year at most, within a couple hours of home.

When we got home, we hugged all three kids tight. I was relieved to be home, and I was eager to sit down and talk with Ava — to set everything straight. I naively thought it would take just a little one-on-one conversation to snap her out of it. That evening, Babak and I told our other two children to go to their rooms so we could sit down with Ava. We were in our family room, she and I on opposite ends of the couch, her dad across the room. I looked over and saw the same child that I'd had before I left for Thailand: T-shirt, sweatpants, a mop of messy, pink-tinted hair.

About a year before, she had started dyeing her hair different colors. First we dyed it blue at the beginning of eighth grade. Schoolmates loved the blue, and it got a lot of attention. Then we colored it red, then purple, then pink. Each successive color change got less attention, and Ava loved attention. She was a middle child who craved a way to stand out. I understood that because I was a middle child myself, growing up dark-skinned between two fair-skinned sisters, and always feeling the need to say, "Look at me."

Ava had always used her wicked intelligence and knowledge to stand out, but people got tired of that. Anytime she didn't get the attention she needed, it would set off a sadness that seemed out of proportion to the situation. I was tired of her constant cycles of needing attention followed by depression. I thought that once her *Jeopardy*-level knowledge wasn't getting noticed any longer, she'd moved on to her hair, and now that the hair wasn't getting attention, she was resorting to *this*. Saying she was trans to gain attention took things to a whole new level, and I just wasn't going to stand for it. Now that I was safely back in Los Angeles, my emotions had shifted, from the initial sorrow of being away from her during a crisis to being tired of having to navigate yet another difficult period with her. I wanted to wrap this latest episode up and put it behind us as soon as possible.

"Tell us what is going on," I said.

Ava proceeded to give us a dissertation on being transgender. As I sat there, my mind raced, and I couldn't hear her exact words. It was as if she were the teacher in a Charlie Brown episode, making some *mwa-mwa-mwa* sounds, until I suddenly heard her end with "I'm a girl."

I looked at her with disbelief, forcing myself to pay attention, while she told us that she wanted to start hormones. She cited resources; she mentioned the Trevor Project, a twenty-four-hour confidential suicide hotline for LGBT teens. She presented us with data. I could feel myself tense up with anger. *Why does he have to look up the Trevor Project? Why does he have to pretend that his life is so bad that he needs to consult a suicide help line? He doesn't understand what a hard life is. My teen years were hard, lonely, brutal. I've worked so hard to give them everything I didn't have, to create this family. How dare he try to make this whole thing seem like a bigger deal than it is when it's about his need to get attention.*

This was so typical of Ava, to try to outsmart everyone by telling them that she knew more about a topic than they did, and therefore she was right. But her knowledge of facts was not going to trump my knowledge of her as my child, my thirteen and a half years of mothering her.

While Babak was trying to hear her out, I began my rebuttal. "You can't just wake up and decide to be a girl one day. People who are trans-gender have signs of it starting when they are three or four years old. They don't just suddenly realize that they are trans at thirteen. I'm a pe-diatrician. I know this. I've never seen someone not have any signs of being transgender until they are thirteen years old. And you can't just start taking hormones. You would have to see a therapist and doctors for a few years before any doctor would consider putting you on hormones. No doctor in their right mind would put you on hormones right now. You are not going to just start ninth grade as a girl. That is not going to happen."

This response will remain one of my biggest regrets in life. I had al-ways told Ava, "There is nothing you can't tell me. I'm your mom. I will always love you. You can tell me anything." I'd said it so many times when she'd gone through cycles of depression and we didn't know the cause. I suspected abuse or bullying that she was scared to reveal. I would prod: "If someone is making you keep secrets and telling you that if you tell us, they'll hurt your family, that's not true. Tell me. I know there is some-thing. You can tell me anything."

She'd reply with, "No one is hurting me. I don't know what it is. I don't."

Just nine months earlier, in September 2016, she had told us she was bisexual. She approached Babak in the family room and said she needed to talk to him. When she had told him, he asked, "Do you want to get your mom so we can talk about it together?"

"I wanted to tell you both, but she's in the shower." Once she had de-cided to tell us, the urgency was so great that she couldn't hold it in long enough for me to get out.

"What you told me is okay, but let's still just wait for Mom to get out of the shower, so the three of us can talk together." Babak came upstairs and asked me to come down to the family room when I was dressed. Then Ava told me what she'd already revealed to her dad.

"What does being bisexual mean to you exactly? How do you know?" I asked her.

"When I go on the Instagram explore page, sometimes there are pictures of people without shirts on. I'm attracted to both the pictures of the boys and the girls," she answered.

I felt a sense of relief at the innocence of it. I'm not sure what I had been afraid of hearing. We said it was okay, we were supportive. Although I was worried about kids in school finding out and making her feel even more lonely, I reassured her. I remember saying, "Your body is going through a lot of hormonal changes right now. It's normal for you to have these feelings. And sometimes when people think they are bisexual, they are actually gay, and that would be okay, too." She excitedly texted the few friends who knew, letting them know that her parents were okay with it, saying that we loved her as long as she was a good person.

Yet when she divulged the biggest secret she was holding in, I said, "No, you don't know what you're talking about. We'll get you a therapist. I love you, but no, you are not a girl." *You can tell me anything but that*, my panicked mind was saying. Thinking back to our old conversations, I had readied myself to accept finding out that someone might be abusing her, but I wasn't okay with finding out that she was transgender. At that time, her simply being who she actually was was worse, in my mind, than her being abused. I'm ashamed to admit it, but it is the truth.

I wish I had just sat there and listened. I wish my response had been something like "This is a lot of information for us to process, so give us some time." I don't remember exactly what Babak said, but I recall that he handled it better than I did. His words were a little closer to "Okay, let's explore this" than "No, this is not the case." And I got so angry at him. Angry that his tone had a hint of acceptance rather than my absolute denial. How dare he give her false hope that we would even consider that she might be a girl?

How can you tell your child they can tell you anything, and then, when they do, say no, they're wrong? How can you just shut them down? I've always described myself as a "validator" — someone who can listen to my friends, or to parents of my patients at work, and validate whatever feelings they are having — yet I immediately invalidated my child. I have always said that everyone just wants to be heard, but I didn't hear my own child. I've always claimed to be an open-minded person, yet when it came to my own child, I shut my mind.

But this was more than being taken by surprise; it felt like *Here we go again*. Here we go again with you being difficult and unhappy and not belonging, and I'm tired of having to try to figure you out. We had finally gotten to a point in the last year where Ava seemed happy. After coming out as bisexual, she made friends with more girls and joined musical theater. She was teaching herself to play the piano and made us all listen to the *Hamilton* soundtrack over and over on the way to school. She ran toward the car with a huge smile on her face at pickup time. She was thriving. Finally, there had seemed to be a light at the end of the tunnel of her unhappiness, and now here we were again. We were going back into the darkness, and I was tired of it. I didn't think there was any possibility that this was real. Why on earth would a teenager want to be transgender, the ultimate outsider? I'd spent thirty years feeling like I was on the outside; now all I wanted for my children was to be happy and to feel like they belonged.

And how does a mother not know her child? How can an open, liberal, and informed mother not have a clue that her child is trans? I refused to believe that the child who had taken the greatest portion of my parental energy was the one I knew the least.

But she kept insisting that she was a girl. "I just know, I feel it, I know it."

"How long have you felt like you are a girl?"

"Six months ago I started to feel like something just wasn't right with my body. I couldn't ignore it. It kept getting worse. I went on the internet and started researching 'not feeling right in your body.' Everything I read about being transgender or saw in YouTube videos of transgender people felt like me. I tried to keep ignoring it, but in the last three months, I've just known. I'm sure. Once I realized I'm a girl, everything started to make sense. I can't ignore it. It's there."

Hearing her say she had felt this way for only six months reinforced everything I thought I knew. She'd used the internet to self-diagnose — one of my greatest pet peeves as a physician — and now, at the age of thirteen and a half, she was announcing that she wanted to start hormones. I was not about to consider letting a teenager start hormones, with irreversible effects such as breast tissue growth, based on six months of internet self-diagnosis.

"Like I said, kids who are trans know that something is wrong when they are little. They don't wake up when they are thirteen and think they're in the wrong body. We'll get you a therapist that specializes in this field. We'll see what the therapist says. And no matter what the therapist says, you are not going to start hormones until you are at least eighteen. You'd have to be working with a therapist and doctors for a few years, and everybody would have to be sure before you could start taking hormones."

Her face shut down. She was sad, but this face — looking straight down at the floor and withdrawn — was one that I had seen too many times throughout her childhood to be alarmed by it. I'd seen it too many times to realize that this time it was different. And I was angry that Ava, who usually accepted everything I said without question, wasn't backing down from her stance. I was frustrated that I hadn't been able to come back to Los Angeles and solve everything with one conversation. I was mad that I was going to be the one to have to find her another therapist and drive her to appointments, and mad that parenting responsibilities always seemed to fall disproportionately on my shoulders.

The therapist would obviously meet with her for a few sessions and say, "Honey, you are not trans." It would take a couple of months to clear all this up, I thought, and then we'd move on. I had no idea that I was about to board a rapid-transit train with no return, or that one year later to the day, I'd be the one filling Ava's first estrogen prescription.

CHAPTER 2

IT'S *a* BOY

W ater is swirling around me. Everything is blurry. The next thing
I know, I'm at the side of the pool, sputtering and coughing, in
my dad's arms. This is my first memory. In my parents' family album is
a picture of me by the pool after falling in, my toddler's belly pooching
out in my two-piece bathing suit, a chocolate chip cookie in my hand, so
sometimes I question whether the memory is real or from the picture. But
I think it is real; the sense of confusion and panic is still vivid. In all my
early memories after that, I want to be a mother.

At five or six years old, I'm playing with my Fisher-Price toy house
and characters, and I'm the mommy figure talking to her kids in my
mommy voice. I'm making my cousin Farshad play Barbies with me yet
again, using his GI Joe figures as stand-ins for the Ken dolls I don't have,
although GI Joe only reaches to Barbie's chest. "My Barbie will be the
mommy, you play the daddy with Joe."

After that, I'm in third grade, and when people ask me what I want
to be when I grow up, I answer, "A mom." This is frustrating for my own
mother, whose number one goal in life is for all three of her daughters not
just to graduate from college but to get professional degrees.

When I am in third grade, we are an upper-middle-class family living in one of the more prestigious neighborhoods of Tehran. I have never wanted for anything. I can walk to the mini-mart at the head of our street, grabbing whatever gum or candy I want, and tell the store owner to add it to our family's tab. In school, I'm one of the more popular girls, popularity in Iran being based more on academic standing than on clothes. Even in third grade, there is class rank, and everyone knows the top five students. Although I'm only third in the class, I make up for it with my American roots. I'm the only one in my family to have been born in the United States — in Baltimore, Maryland, while my father was doing his internship before moving on to New York University for his neurology residency. When I was three, our family moved back to Iran. My first memory, of the pool, is from the United States.

My mother was one of eight children, six girls and two boys, and the only one in her family to graduate from college, earning a bachelor's degree in chemistry from the University of Tehran. She is incredibly smart, much smarter and sharper than my dad, by his admission and everyone else's. My parents got married when my mother was nineteen. She finished her degree despite my older sister being born when she was twenty-one. When they moved to the US for my dad's medical training, my mom started graduate school at NYU with a toddler in tow. But then she unexpectedly got pregnant with me, and raising a toddler and a baby while living half a world away from any family support, she was forced to drop out of graduate school. Having never finished her master's degree, she was determined that all three of her daughters would make up for that, and we did. Several years into the Islamic Revolution in Iran, as conditions continued to deteriorate, my parents used my dad's training and my US citizenship to get our family back to the States. My sisters both became lawyers, and I, the one who always wanted to be a mom, became a mother and a pediatrician almost simultaneously.

I've always wondered why my strong desire to be a mother started so early. Maybe it had to do with being a middle child. Maybe I needed love so badly that I wanted my own children to give it to and give it back. But that doesn't really make sense. I played mother before my younger sister was born, before I was a middle child. And my parents and my extended family gave me plenty of love and attention. I was always very sensitive, a vulnerability my mom's younger sister, Shaheen, had picked up on. She made it a point to dote on me, making me feel like the most special of her numerous nieces and nephews. In Iranian culture, where white skin is synonymous with beauty, she knew I had picked up on the murmurings around me that contrasted my dark skin with that of my two fair-skinned sisters. Once I overheard a friend tell my mother, "You shouldn't let her ride her bike in the street all day while the sun is out. She gets so dark so easily."

My mom shut down these negative comments, but my Aunt Shaheen was the one who reassured me. "I would give anything for your chocolate-colored skin," she'd tell me. "In America, people go on expensive vacations and lay out in the sun to get your skin, but people in Iran are not sophisticated enough to know that." Then she'd tell me stories about the brief time she lived in America, chasing love and a relationship with a boyfriend that didn't work out.

Maybe I wanted my own baby to dote on, the way Shaheen doted on me, making me feel secretly special and protected. Maybe some people just have stronger maternal instincts than others. Whatever the underlying reason, my maternal instinct has always been powerful, and motherhood is a stronger part of my identity than being a physician, a wife, or any of the other roles I've had.

Babak and I met during our first year of medical school — or before it. We first saw each other at the medical school orientation party at Peter's Pub in Pittsburgh and only said a couple of words to each other. I already had a boyfriend, and Babak had no interest in someone who looked like what he called a "typical high-maintenance Iranian princess." When I started drifting apart from my boyfriend, our mutual friend Prathima kept suggesting that I get to know Babak, despite my insistence that he wasn't my type. Since the orientation party, the only times I'd seen him outside class were in the anatomy lab, hunched over a cadaver. I'd gone to the anatomy lab after hours only twice all semester, and he'd been there both times. "All he does is study. If he's been there both times that I've gone in after hours, then you know he is there every night," I told Prathima, rolling my eyes.

"He's actually really funny," she insisted. "Just talk to him for five minutes, and if you don't like him, I'll let it go." We were at the Attic for a postexam party, and it was the first time I had seen Babak at a social event since orientation. Wearing his big wire-rimmed glasses and holding a beer, he was sitting on a stool, where I reluctantly walked up to him. I have no idea what my opening line was. We talked until the Attic closed down at 3 a.m., and then he walked me home. A few weeks later, I gave my boyfriend the "It's not you, it's me" talk.

Once Babak and I started dating, it wasn't long before I laid out my plans. "Listen, I want to have at least four kids, and I don't plan to work more than part time. Being a mom is always going to be my first priority. If you don't think you want at least four kids, we probably should break up before we get too deep into this relationship."

Babak was young; he hadn't really thought about kids and didn't necessarily want any. "Can we just adopt a seventeen-year-old Swedish girl and send her to college the next year?" he joked, but he agreed to having kids. I'm a planner. I planned everything, and at that time, he was happy to comply.

Having determined that he was on board with having kids, I decided to fill him in on the rest of my life plans. My kids were going to grow up in LA, where they would avoid the loneliness and bigotry that I'd experienced. Part of my loneliness during my difficult teen years was likely due to being one of the only brown kids in our Pittsburgh suburb of Mt. Lebanon, but maybe a larger part was self-imposed, after my self-confidence was shattered in fifth grade.

After the Iran-Iraq War started, the quality of the education system in Iran began to decline, particularly for women. My parents were determined that their daughters should have no limits on their education, so they left their very comfortable life in Tehran to come to the US and start from scratch. We landed in Madison, Wisconsin, because I had a maternal aunt living there, and I started fifth grade in the fall of 1983.

It was shortly after the Iran hostage crisis. I spent that school year getting taunted every day. My seat was toward the back of the classroom, where I was surrounded by a group of boys who called me "dark and dirty" and told me, "Go back to where you came from." I'd sit in class trying to blink back my tears while discreetly removing the spitballs from my hair that came from every direction. I can still feel shivers up my spine from their whispers, still feel the moistness on my fingertips. I spent every recess and lunch period in hiding. At night I begged my parents to send me back home, but I didn't tell them what was happening at school. I'd just say I missed my friends and family at home. I blocked most of that year from my memory, not recalling certain scenes until thirty years later, when I'd get visions of them while I was running.

I rarely forget a face, but I can't remember the face of almost anyone from that school year. I remember my fourth-grade teacher in Tehran and my sixth-grade teacher in Pittsburgh, but I don't know if my fifth-grade teacher was a man or a woman. Whoever that teacher was, they must have known what was happening in the back of that classroom, yet they did nothing to stop it.

Fortunately, my father got a job in Pittsburgh, and we left Madison before I started sixth grade. And while my classmates in Pittsburgh were much nicer, the damage was done. That faceless year in Madison left a lasting imprint on me, one that in some way influences every decision I make. I was a minority carrying all that hate and fear with me. I was never able to fully integrate.

A few years later, my aunt moved to Los Angeles, and we started visiting her regularly. I'd seen plenty of diversity and felt more comfortable in my skin on our regular visits to New York City, but the Westwood neighborhood of Los Angeles — nicknamed Tehrangeles for its large population of Iranians — felt more familiar. I was already imagining my future family. Now I envisioned us living in LA, where my children would blend in and never be outsiders as I had been. So after Babak agreed to having kids, I also soon let him know, "Once all our medical training is done, I want us to settle in LA." He wasn't initially sold on leaving the East Coast. Babak was born in Esfahān, but his family had moved to the US in 1978, when he was just five. He grew up in the suburbs of Philadelphia and studied fine arts and chemistry at the University of Pennsylvania. He had never been west of Pittsburgh, and before we started dating, he had every intention of moving back to Main Line Philadelphia.

We visited LA together for my cousin's wedding, and I took him to Gladstones in Malibu. We sat at an outside table by the beach, the smell of the ocean air around us, the wind in our hair. Pelicans flew and squawked all around us while we ate and drank. He was sold.

Of course, by the time Babak first saw me at the orientation party, I wasn't that awkward girl from middle school anymore. In college, I had regained a good part of my confidence. I found my tribe. I made some girlfriends, I had my first drink, and then I had one too many fifty-cent screwdrivers on ladies' night at Chauncey's where the men were every flavor of cheese. I expressed myself through fashion; I went on dates. The guys who had once preferred the safety of dating the high school cheerleaders were now also out of high school and not bound by its social rules. It seemed like overnight, I had become exotic rather than the girl you wouldn't dare to date. While my girlfriend was on the dance floor, I stood at the bar by myself in my lace top and platform shoes, my hair to my waist and my winged eyeliner exaggerating the shape of my eyes. When the guys yelled over the blaring music, "Where are you from?," I confidently hollered back that I was Iranian, feeling a sense of thrill and power as their eyes widened. I was making it my mission to show that not all Iranian girls observed hijab; they could be just like any other partying Americans. And while I enjoyed this new persona, I did not lose sight of my vision of my future family.

Two years into our marriage, I announced my first pregnancy fairly early on to everyone. We were living in Cleveland, Ohio, and I was in my second year of my pediatrics residency. I desperately wanted daughters, and I assumed that this baby was a girl. Everything else had gone according to my plan. "Are you going to find out what you're having?" friends would ask.

"Yes, I'll find out. But I know it's a girl. This body only makes girls." Mind you, I had a medical degree, and knew all about X and Y chromosomes when I made these ridiculous proclamations. But I truly believed this about my body. To say I was surprised when my ultrasound technician said, "It's a boy!" is an understatement. Things had not gone according to plan.

Mother's Day was two days after my ultrasound. My younger sister, Parimah, had given me a card that said, "Of all the babies to be, yours is the luckiest one to have you for a mom." I burst into tears, declaring, "This baby is not lucky at all. I don't know anything about how to raise boys. I don't know how to play baseball." Babak and my mom looked at each other, as if they had been waiting for this moment.

"I'm so excited," my mom said. "This is the first boy in our family." My dad used to joke that even our family cat, Hannah, was a girl. "You're going to be the best mom."

Babak put his arms around me and reassured me. "Besides, I know how to play baseball. I need to make some contribution to this kid's life."

Once I'd said it out loud and had a little pity party for myself, I moved on. For a few days I was sad and a little worried about how I was actually going to raise a boy, but I was back to being excited pretty soon. After all, this was my first pregnancy, and I was only twenty-eight. The next one would be a girl.

While I knew all about chromosomes, I knew very little about gender and genitalia. I'm not even sure I had ever heard the word *transgender*. *Transvestite*, yes; *transgender*, no. (The term *transvestite*, which I had heard before, is no longer used; the term *cross-dressing* is used instead.)

In medical school in the late 1990s, and even during pediatric residency training at the Cleveland Clinic Foundation, a major urban medical institution, from 1999 to 2002, not once did I hear the word *transgender*.

Despite my disappointment over my pregnancy with a boy, it was love at first sight when I laid eyes on my firstborn son, whom we named Armon, all snug and wrapped in the pink and blue hospital blankets. It would be a full sixteen years before I made the connection between the pink, blue, and white stripes of the trans pride flag and the baby blankets newborns are wrapped in. Motherhood proved to be so much more rewarding and all-encompassing than I had ever imagined, fulfilling the sense of identity I had been seeking for years. By the time Armon was fifteen months old, I was ready to try for that next baby. Surely number two would be a girl.

I got pregnant quickly, and this pregnancy was very different. While pregnant with Armon, I'd experienced occasional nausea and fatigue. Several times during hospital rounds I had to excuse myself to go vomit and return a few minutes later as if nothing had happened. But with my second, I didn't have just morning sickness: I had all-day sickness and vomited multiple times a day. *Something is definitely different*, I thought. I eventually gave in and started taking the antiemetic Zofran prescribed by my obstetrician, and as I kept losing weight, added Reglan, hoping its gut-motility stimulation effects would add some benefit. Several times in those first few months, Babak brought home IV fluids from the hospital and we would run them at night, getting me hydrated enough to go to work the next day. At one OB appointment, my doctor looked at all the bruises from the IV placement attempts in my dehydrated arms and asked what was going on. "I'm not being abused, the Zofran and Reglan are just not cutting it." I weighed less than I did in high school. On the worst night, I was throwing up more fluid than I was gaining intravenously. Babak was exasperated, suggesting we just go to the hospital for me to have an abortion. I told him he was crazy. "Who aborts a child that is a pregnancy they planned?" Fortunately, at about sixteen weeks, things finally turned around.

By my twenty-week ultrasound, I was feeling normal again. While during my hyperemesis gravidarum phase (severe nausea and vomiting during pregnancy), I'd thought I just might be having a girl, now I started to worry I'd be having another boy. This time, when the ultrasound technician used her cursor to outline the penis and testicles on the screen and say, "It's a boy! One hundred percent!," I was sad but not surprised. I remember going out for a birthday dinner with Babak, sad to be turning thirty and sad to be having my second boy.

A couple of months after Ava came out to us as transgender, I kept remembering that thirtieth birthday, feeling guilty that somehow I had caused all of this. Maybe karma was real. I blamed myself for being so stupid when I was thirty, but eventually I let go of that blame. After all, the moment she was born, as I heard the nurse assisting my doctor taking a look at her genitals and again declaring, "It's a boy!," the moment I heard her beautiful voice cry, I was instantly in love with my baby, as much as the first time — penis, testicles, and all.

CHAPTER 3

NOT MY DAUGHTER

The morning after our return from Thailand, light streaming through my Los Angeles bedroom window meant I could finally stop trying to sleep and get my jet-lagged body out of bed. I felt like I had the worst hangover of my life, frustration and worry being the toxins causing it. Recalling the previous night's conversation, I knew I had to honor my promise to find Ava an LGBT therapist as soon as possible.

June was already going to be a really busy month. Adding "find and schedule therapist" to my long postvacation to-do lists filled me with resentment. First I had to go to the fifth-grade graduation, or "culmination" as they called it, for our youngest child — our daughter, Shayda — on May 30, followed by Ava's eighth-grade awards ceremony and graduation on June 1. Ava received six academic achievement awards, and as she stood on the podium accepting each award from Mr. Wilson, she looked happy and proud. *It's all going to be fine*, I thought. *He is happy and smiling, and clearly he just can't handle me being away from home. I just need to give him the attention he needs, and he'll forget all about this.*

For the evening graduation ceremony, Ava had to wear the required boys' attire, a suit, under the graduation gown. I gave her the dark navy suit with fine light-blue stripes that Armon had worn for his eighth-grade graduation, although it was a little big. It took her forever to put it on, and I kept telling her to hurry up so we'd have time to take some pictures before we left. She eventually came downstairs looking miserable. She didn't want to take pictures. "Everyone takes graduation day pictures. Smile, and don't make it look fake," I commanded. After the ceremony, where she was the only graduate there with bright-pink hair, we took more pictures. She had a fake smile in all of them. I was irritated that after seeming happy at the awards ceremony in the morning, she was now acting upset again. Now, when I look back at the pictures, I notice one in particular of the two of us in the backyard, in which she appears so uncomfortable that it almost looks like spiders are crawling up the back of her jacket. But what could I have done? She wasn't ready to come out, and the boys were required to wear suits. I suppose we could have skipped graduation altogether, or at least I could have been a little more sympathetic — I could have acknowledged and validated her discomfort.

I started investigating therapists. First, I turned to the Los Angeles LGBT center in West Hollywood. All the therapists on their list for teens were far from our home, so they suggested I contact an organization called Colors, based at Antioch University, that provided free therapy for LGBT youth. It was staffed by students who had already completed their psychology degrees and were getting further training, specifically in LGBT issues. I remember thinking it was ironic that as a pediatrician practicing in LA, I had a hard time finding therapists even for kids and teens who were covered by insurance, yet it was apparently easy to get free therapy if you were LGBT.

I emailed Colors through their website and received a call from the program director. I explained Ava's situation to him, calling her "my son," who I thought was gay but confused. "He thinks he is a girl, but has never before the age of thirteen had any signs of being one. And we would know. It's not like we are closed-minded parents. I'm a pediatrician. I work with kids and teens. And my husband has a lot of transgender clients."

For several years now, Babak had been performing transgender top surgery, which entails either removing breasts and creating a male-contoured chest for someone assigned female at birth who identifies as male, or placing breast implants in someone who is assigned male at birth and identifies as female (after they've been on hormone therapy for at least eighteen months). One of my theories was that Ava might be saying she was trans to get her dad's attention, because what were the chances that a doctor who does transgender top surgery, which not many doctors do, would actually have a child who is transgender?

The director listened to my assessment patiently and without judgment. "We're not parents who have forced gender roles on our kids. For example, he has never been sporty, so we've never forced sports on him."

Ava played soccer with the Associated Youth Soccer Organization for a few seasons and didn't enjoy it. We gave her the option of pulling out early, after maybe one season, but she decided to continue for a few seasons before saying she didn't want to do it anymore. Armon and Ava both did one semester of tae kwon do, and neither of them liked it much, so we pulled them out. Ava never showed an interest in any other sports. Later she took tennis lessons, and although she was okay at it, she didn't like it enough to continue. Sometimes the tennis instructor would tell her to run less like a ballerina on the court so she could get around faster. He didn't mean it as any kind of gendered slur; he was referring to her distinctive style of tiptoe running and walking, dating from when she was a toddler. Plenty of boys are not into sports, plenty of girls are, so we never thought her lack of interest in sports reflected gender — it was just who Ava was.

The director finally interjected, "I have a therapist in mind who I think would be a good match for your family. I'll pass on your information, and the therapist will call you directly to find a time that works for both of you." The next day, I got a call from Hope.

"Hi, this is Hope. I'm calling from Colors. Is this Aydin's mom?" My heart skipped a few beats. She had a very kind demeanor and gentle voice, but it was a deep, masculine-sounding voice. *Oh my God*, I thought, *they assigned us a transgender therapist?*

I had told Ava I would find her an appropriate therapist who specialized in gender identity issues, but did that person really need to be trans? I was ambivalent. Would a trans person "push" being trans on her rather than really listening to Ava's entire history to figure out what was going on? Then I berated myself for my ridiculous thoughts. Presumably Hope was a professional. And if she was trans, then it wouldn't take many appointments for Hope to declare, "Aydin is not trans but just confused, a gay boy who wants to explore his feminine side."

I tried to give Hope a summary of Ava's childhood, along with my assessment of why Ava might be saying she was trans. "As a toddler, he was a really happy kid," I began. "He was obsessed with Hot Wheels and trains." Using the term *obsessed* was not an exaggeration. Armon had been all about superheroes, so Batman and all his friends were scattered throughout our house. But after someone brought a pack of Hot Wheels for the kids as a present, Ava would not go anywhere without a Hot Wheel in each hand and a few in her pockets. Whether napping during the day or sleeping at night, she always took a few into her crib. In one of my favorite pictures from Halloween, she is in a pumpkin costume, crying but clinging to a Hot Wheel in each hand.

The first time she was distracted by other toys, to the point of having me hold her cars for her, was when she saw the big train table at a children's museum. She played with the trains for an hour, taking them around and around the track, under tunnels and over bridges. Following her interest, I filled our house with Thomas the Tank Engine and all his friends. I learned to tell Thomas apart from Gordon, Percy apart from Henry.

"And it's not like he wasn't exposed to girl toys, because I have a younger daughter, so tea sets and princess costumes have always been in our home. He has never had an interest in them," I told Hope. "I just think that as a middle child, he has always been starving for attention. He's had a hard time finding his place. He's spent years being depressed for no reason, and that is the root of the problem."

Hope listened patiently, without any judgment in her tone, and

Ava in her pumpkin costume, crying but clinging to a Hot Wheel in each
hand, standing next to Armon in his Batman costume.

without giving any particular feedback. She proposed an appointment
that Monday, June 19, at 7 p.m. We were scheduled to go to Cancun for
a five-day trip the next day with our family friends. Did I really want to
schedule this first appointment before this much-needed vacation? Even
though I had just come back from a yoga retreat, I was feeling anything
but rested. We had planned the family trip to Cancun after we booked our
Thailand trip, feeling guilty and wanting to make sure we spent at least
a few quality days with the kids. But I accepted the appointment. *The
sooner we get started, the sooner we can put this behind us.*

At our appointment, the woman at the sign-in desk in the lobby
looked back and forth between our faces and asked who the appointment
was for. "It's for my son," I answered, but then scribbled my own name

illegibly. I wanted to protect Ava, from what exactly I wasn't sure...from someone finding out she was getting therapy there, I guess. We rode the elevator up in silence and found space on a loveseat. The waiting room was filled with flyers about LGBT meetings, support groups, marriage counseling, and domestic violence. The magazines were mostly *Family Circle* and *Better Homes and Gardens*. There were no trans or LGBT magazines.

One by one, therapists opened the waiting room door and gently nodded at their clients to follow them in. When the door opened again, I knew it was Hope before she looked down at her folder and called out, "Aydin?"

Yes, she was definitely transgender. Even if her voice had not already betrayed her on the phone, it only took one glance at her to know. She brought me a clipboard with some intake forms to fill out.

Hope was wearing leggings and a flowy top that wasn't quite long enough to cover her groin area. I immediately thought that she must have tucked her genitals, unless she had already had gender reassignment surgery. It sounds terrible that this was one of the first things that I noticed about her, when it is the exact opposite of how I would ever want people to look at my child, but it's the truth. Her hair was almost shoulder length; she was clearly growing it out, thin and wispy and light mousy brown. Her foundation covered a hint of gray stubble underneath. She had on a long necklace that went well with her outfit, and she was wearing soft and comfortable-looking ballet flats. She was quite tall, maybe six feet. I guessed that she was in her late thirties or possibly early forties.

We sat down in her office and talked. Although I liked her warmth and her gentle, kind voice, no amount of soothing tone could hide the bass underneath it. I didn't want this future for my child — this future where the first thing people would notice about her, before they noticed the warmth in her eyes, the radiance in her smile, the complex brilliance of her mind, the goodness of her heart, was that she was trans.

We went over the intake and consent forms briefly, and then I was dismissed to the waiting room. When we first saw Hope together, I detected a glimmer of hope, or relief, or happiness, or a combination of all three, in my daughter's face. Now I think that maybe it was a look of recognition: *Oh, this is my person.*

I don't remember much about that fifty-minute wait for Ava to come back out. Although I had taken a book with me, I was unable to read it. I was the only person in the silent waiting room. I randomly flipped through some magazines, checked my social media feed a few times, paced the little room. My heart rate was just a little accelerated for the entire fifty minutes, and I felt nauseated. My baby was in there and being influenced by someone I didn't know. My baby... my baby who had been difficult from the moment she was born.

During my brief attempt at being a crafty Martha Stewart mom, I had made Ava's birth announcements myself. I had captured a picture of her in mid-scream, hair sticking up like a porcupine. I posted it on a striped blue background and tied a baby-blue ribbon on top. The picture was representative of her temperament up to that point. She was colicky, and for months the only way to soothe her was to have her latched onto me or to rock her. But I didn't mind her difficult newborn phase. Seeing newborns has always been my favorite part of my job — I love their distinctive cry, their silky soft skin, their intoxicating, milky aroma.

The waiting room door finally opened.

"Aydin says you guys will be back from Cancun by Sunday, so I'll see you again next week, same time. You can text me if for some reason you are delayed." Hope smiled at me and ducked back into the private therapy zone. No feedback. Nothing.

Ava was happy. Not radiantly happy, but the kind of happiness that puts a small smile on your face as your mind clearly replays something. While we walked back to our car, I took quick glances at her face and then looked ahead again. I can't remember what we talked about on the car ride home. I probably asked her if she liked the session, and I'm sure she said yes. We both commented that Hope seemed nice. I remember thinking at some point that Hope was lovely. I would be happy to have her as my friend. We could go to lunch and each have a glass of rosé and share a pasta and a salad like I would do with any other girlfriend. I just wouldn't want her to be my future adult daughter.

On each visit, Hope had on the same type of outfit. She always wore leggings, a loose hip-length top, ballet flats, and jewelry. *This must be what works for her*, I thought. *This must be the female outfit that works best with her broad shoulders and thin legs.* Sometimes I wondered if she wore something different when she wasn't working, or if this was just her go-to outfit for all occasions. Once during a conversation with me, she said, "I'm still transitioning." Now I wondered when she would consider her transition complete.

After that first appointment with Hope, when Ava seemed secretly happy, I was angry again. Part of me probably hoped it would only take one session to call this whole thing off, like an impulsive wedding you rush into for no reason and then call off. When we got home, Babak said he didn't want to hear anything about it. "We're leaving for Cancun in the morning. I just want to go on vacation and enjoy these five days before facing reality. I don't want anything to ruin this vacation, and it's not like anything is going to happen over the next five days anyway." This was one of the times that I desperately needed to talk, but Babak couldn't. His timeline and way of processing emotions are different from mine. And since I'm not someone who can hold things in, just a couple of days into our vacation, I told my friend Eileen everything.

We were in the pool, rosé or margarita or frozen daiquiri in hand, when I began, "You won't believe what he's up to this time." If she was surprised or shocked, she didn't show it. "I know of two families in our school who are going through the same thing," Eileen said. "Maybe you want to talk to them? I can put you in touch." Again I felt angry. Why was it that anyone I confided in considered that Ava's being trans was a real possibility? When I had told our friend Jake everything at the retreat, he'd had a similar reaction: "Wow, that's a lot, but it could be real." He had been in our home and around Ava a lot. Eileen had known Ava since she was three. I needed them to say that they were sorry that my kid was putting me through all this bullshit and that raising teens is hard. I didn't want to hear from them that there might actually be truth to what Ava was telling me.

Left to right: **Armon, Shayda, and Ava as children.**

I grilled Eileen. "But have you ever thought for one second that Aydin might be a girl?"

"No, I never have. But I also don't know anything about this. These other parents may be able to help you."

"I don't need to talk to parents with trans kids, because I don't have a trans kid!"

I argued that we had been in Cancun for two days already, and Ava hadn't shaved, letting the stubble grow on her face. She hadn't even bothered bringing a razor. If she was really trans, wouldn't having stubble bother her more than anything else? Wouldn't she shave every day? I used this argument as 100 percent complete proof that she was not a girl. Eileen agreed that she found it odd that Ava wouldn't bring a razor but reiterated that she really didn't know anything about this. She was happy to listen to me anytime and have me cry to her, she said, but if at any point I changed my mind, she was also happy to connect me with these other families. This suggestion was the first time in eleven years of friendship that I felt she was letting me down.

Overall, we had a great trip. We always had a good time together as a family, and those five days felt like exactly what we needed. But on our way back from Cancun, Ava was already looking forward to her appointment with Hope the next day.

I found it deeply frustrating that I had to sit in the waiting room during these appointments and not have a clue what was going on between Hope and Ava. It was now July 2017, and Ava started a three-week day camp with Shayda and my friend Juliet's kids. The camp was at the Summer Arts Academy, about fifteen miles east of our home — at least an hour's drive each way, so no other kids from our neighborhood were attending. The camp offered classes in art, music, theater, and cinematography. Ava and Shayda had a great time, meeting kids from new neighborhoods to the east of us. It was also where Ava met Cora.

Cora went to the Larchmont Charter School. She and Ava became instant friends, and she was one of the first people that Ava came out to. One day, Ava came home from camp with dark blue nail polish on one hand. I noticed it, but said nothing; it could just have been a fun, punk thing to do, so I wasn't going to make it a big deal. Although I don't remember asking about it, I do remember her telling me at some point that she had had Cora paint her nails only on one hand. For some reason Ava thought that would upset me less than having both hands painted. Then she started asking to buy some of the clothes that Cora was wearing.

These were mainly overalls, which had come back into fashion for girls. I told her I thought overalls were cute, and there was nothing particularly feminine or masculine about them. "But the overalls I want are the ones in the girls' section," Ava said.

"Overalls are overalls. If you prefer the ones in the girls' section, that's fine, but you'll need to just try them on first and make sure they fit okay in the crotch area. They may be cut differently. If they fit okay, I'll buy them for you." I was hoping to convey that it was okay to explore clothes and paint your nails, and these things didn't make you a girl. I told her that in the eighties, all the guys in bands wore makeup and experimented with fashion. Duran Duran and Culture Club had helped me get through my lonely preteen and teen years. I used to watch MTV for hours waiting for a Duran Duran video to come up, and I fantasized about a relationship with John Taylor after seeing the "Hungry Like the Wolf" video.

Once I'd okayed the overalls, Ava showed me some dresses at H&M that she wanted to buy and wear with leggings. They were really just oversized, knee-length T-shirts. I told her I had to show them to her dad first. Babak and I decided we should not make a big deal out of the things she was asking for, which were really more gender-neutral than feminine. We were going along with this whole gender-neutral self-expression thing, and continuing to see Hope weekly, and I kept deluding myself that soon enough Ava would either get over the trans thing or just realize that she could be a boy and still have fun with fashion and be happy with that. And then, within a month, I had a big wake-up call.

Mondays, which were my day off from work, had gone from being my favorite day of the week to the worst day. In LA traffic, it took us a good forty-five minutes at least to get to Antioch University for our appointments. We always left the house right around 6 p.m., and by the time we got home, it was usually close to 9 p.m. I spent my entire day off dreading the time in traffic, and even worse, the time sitting in the waiting room. I'd given up on trying to take a book to read while I waited. My heart continued to beat just a little faster during her entire session.

On that day, I spent my typical fifty minutes in the waiting room looking at the various posters and pamphlets. Do you suffer from domestic violence? Are you trans masculine and interested in a support group? I wondered again how the hell I had ended up there. I scrolled through my phone and social media feed and flipped through a couple of magazines until Hope opened the door of the waiting room, waved, and said, "See you next week." That was it. Again, no feedback — no "This is what I think may be going on," or "Can I talk to you for a few minutes now?" Frustration kept building up. *This is my child. Why doesn't anyone ever understand that?*

We started walking back to the car. Ava was wearing sweatpants and a T-shirt. Her colored hair was tousled and messy on the top of her head as usual. She looked like any other thirteen-year-old boy, other than her nails. She'd moved on from the dark, punk-style color on one hand to bright pink on both. Her nails were the only clue and act of defiance to tell the world something was going on.

As we got in the car, I noticed how beautiful the clouds looked in the sky. At least it was summer and not dark yet. I hated to think that in a few months I'd have to make this drive both ways in the dark. Ava and I were both quiet and tired. And then just as I was about to merge onto the 405, she said, "Mom, I need to tell you something." Then she pulled up the left leg of her sweatpants. "I shaved my legs."

I felt like I had just plummeted down the steep fall of a roller coaster. My head was spinning, and I wanted to throw up. I heard myself telling

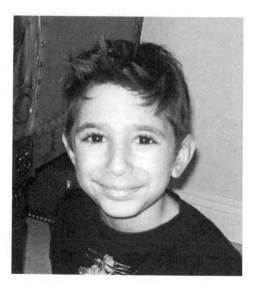

Ava as a child.

myself to focus on the highway and not get into an accident. *Calm down, calm down, calm down,* I kept thinking. *Don't let him see how shocked and horrified you are.*

This was the first time that Ava had ever done anything without asking my permission. This was my child who was scared of doing anything on her own for fear of messing it up. She couldn't make a peanut butter sandwich without explicit directions, for fear of using too much or too little peanut butter or using the wrong knife, so for her to figure out how to take a razor and shave her legs on her own meant that this was no longer a joke or something I could ignore. This wasn't something that would go away.

"Why did you shave your legs?" I demanded.

"Because it's the next step in being a girl. To shave my arms and legs."

"Who told you that?"

"I talked to Hope about what I could do to start feeling more comfortable with my body. She said that eventually, this would be the next step."

I was fuming inside. I knew it. I knew I shouldn't have let Hope be her therapist. *Of course a trans woman would just get him to do what he needs to do to be trans, rather than actually ask him the appropriate questions and delve into his past to see why the hell he thinks he is trans or why the hell he has never been happy for no fucking reason and needed attention. I fucking tried to be politically correct and not object to a trans therapist rather than think of what's in the best interest of my child, and now this.*

I kept driving. My jaw was clenched. "I'm going to have to tell your dad."

"Okay, but is that all you have to say about it?"

I didn't answer.

"You're just having a hard time because your daughter is sitting here next to you telling you what she is going through, and you can't accept it." Hearing her use the word *daughter* for the first time, I felt like I had just been whipped with a belt. *You are not my daughter,* I thought in my head. *I have a daughter at home. I have a daughter and I have two sons.* I said nothing.

We drove the rest of the way home in silence, the tension in the car so thick you could cut it with a knife. When we got home, I had Babak come to our bedroom. I told him this was serious, and therapy was not working. It was time to start looking for a new therapist, one who wasn't going to "push the trans agenda," one who was going to look at our kid as a whole. I wanted a therapist who was going to take into account everything I told them about my child's past, one who would address whatever the underlying issue was that made her depressed, rather than just focusing on her latest obsession. I also felt that I needed to be more involved in the sessions and get updates on what was transpiring in them. I needed a therapist who would give me more feedback. Although I had brought up this issue with Hope several times, she had told me that she could not do it yet.

We agreed that I would tell Hope that with school starting in the fall, the distance to her office was too much, so that after a few more sessions, we'd switch to a therapist closer to our home.

During those first few months of my denial, I found out that Ava had been going on Reddit and asking questions. Ava and I were arguing about some aspect of being transgender, and she said, "Well, I asked on Reddit, and the general answer was —"

"What is Reddit?" I demanded.

I was angry. I was upset that Ava was going on social media and publicly saying that she was trans or questioning her gender, even anonymously, because how anonymous is anything on social media? I was afraid she would develop an online friendship with some sort of sexual predator that would endanger not only her but also her siblings or the rest of the family. I was upset that yet again she had defied me, as she had by shaving her legs. My child who didn't do anything without asking me was now doing things behind my back that she knew I did not want her to do. I mentioned to Hope that I did not want Ava asking questions of random people on an online platform and that I thought it was unsafe.

Later, I heard Ava describe the first time she shaved her legs, saying she felt this sudden euphoria with the first pass of the razor. She described feeling like a caterpillar shedding, finding herself and her smooth body under this thick hair that came with puberty and didn't feel like hers. She felt relief that she might still exist underneath it all.

I remembered the first time I shaved my own legs. My mom had said I was not allowed to, but I was the only girl in sixth grade not shaving her legs. I already stood out from all the other girls enough, and the hair on my legs was so thick and dark compared to the smooth legs of my blonde classmates. Once I'd shaved, I wore shorts to school, then tried to keep my legs out of view on the car ride home and changed into sweatpants immediately once we got home. One day, I forgot to change. I was standing close to my mom and caught her glancing at my legs. My heart started racing. She didn't say anything. She must have known I was shaving, but she never chose to acknowledge that I was doing it or tell me it was okay. After that, I continued to shave my legs without hiding them. My mom and I never talked about it. Just as Ava was making her statement by shaving her legs, I had felt the need to make my own.

During all this turmoil, running was my saving grace. I had started running about five years earlier, going from not being able to run a mile to running two marathons in the previous year. I had turned to running at a time when I felt like I was drowning, when my multiple identities of mother, doctor, wife, daughter, friend, sister, and colleague had started to overwhelm me and at times, it felt like I couldn't breathe. I felt that I was doing everything for everyone else and nothing for myself. I decided to train for a half marathon, to use that goal to at least get back in shape and reclaim my body. After the first three to four months of torturous running, it gradually became my therapy. All my unresolved feelings about identity and grief over my Aunt Shaheen's unexpected early death came up, and often I found myself crying on my runs, sweat, tears, and snot mingling and streaming down my face. After my first half marathon, I continued to run, craving my run-therapy sessions, my moving meditation.

While running, I found words and thoughts and ideas swirling around in my head. When I got home, I grabbed a pen and whatever junk mail was around and scribbled down the words that had come to me during my run. Those words inspired me to start writing, leading to a blog called *Mom on the Runsanity: A Journey of Running and Writing*. I wrote under the pretext of chronicling my marathon training, but I was really writing about life, about losing myself in motherhood and then finding myself again on the run. In a post called "Marriage, the Marathon," I compared marathon training to the ups and downs of a long-term marriage, both with finish lines we are not certain we will cross. I submitted that entry to the magazine *Women's Running*. It was published, and I began making regular contributions to the magazine's website.

I wrote about my Aunt Shaheen's death, about being bullied in fifth grade, and about my high school experience. Eventually, after seeing some hateful anti-Iranian, pro-Trump commentary on Facebook, in a post titled "Immigrant" I wrote the words that were hardest for me to admit:

> I've also realized that I have spent thirty years trying to prove to everyone around me that I am just like them…that I am just one of them…that you and I are the same…but we are not. Never has it been more clear to me than today that being an immigrant has affected every single decision I've made in some way…that no matter how much I've tried to suppress my experience, being an immigrant has shaped who I am today…and it will therefore continue to impact every decision I make.

After Ava came out, it was hard for me to continue to write my blog. I couldn't share what was happening in Ava's life, and I couldn't write about myself without mentioning an event that had taken over my life and mind. But while my writing slowed, my running continued. My runs were the only time I felt that everything would be all right eventually. My legs became slower, my body weighed down by the racing thoughts that had taken over my mind. I logged more slow and tear-filled miles than ever.

My favorite quote for years had been from Isak Dinesen: "The cure for anything is salt water: sweat, tears, or sea." After I ran my first marathon, my blog post title had been "Sweat, Tears, Sea," and for a couple of years I had been thinking of getting those words tattooed inside my wrist. On my forty-fourth birthday, amid all the uncertainty about what was going on with Ava, I decided it was time. I needed this permanent reminder that everything would be okay, that as long as I continued to run, I could handle anything, and all the answers would eventually reveal themselves. And so on July 11, 2017, at the same time that Ava started to shave her legs, I got my first and only tattoo: Sweat, Tears, Sea.

Back when I was blogging about life and running, I wrote about Caitlyn Jenner after watching a TV interview with her, but I related my piece to running, having no clue that I had a trans daughter. Caitlyn (formerly known as Bruce) was an Olympic gold-medal-winning decathlete who had just come out as a trans woman. Contrasting the way Jenner had used athletics to run away from herself to prove her manhood with my choice to use running to rediscover myself, I had said that I hoped people were using running to run toward and not away from themselves. I declared how happy I was that Jenner could finally stop running away and at last find herself. Back then I had no idea that my story would eventually become a trans story.

In a blog post called "Born," written the week after my nephew was born and gay marriage became legal, I wrote that my kids knew that some people are straight, or gay, or born in the wrong body — that these states of being are different. At the time, I had no idea that these ideas directly applied to one of my own kids. The possibility of one of our boys being gay was something we thought about occasionally because our boys were both such sensitive kids. But aren't all little boys like that? What do we do in raising them that tells them they shouldn't continue to be sensitive or show their emotions, that big boys and men don't do that? All the little boys I have taken care of over the years have been sweet and sensitive. When does that change, and why, and how?

But while I was always accepting of trans people in principle, it seemed that I was not okay with my own child being trans. Was that all just because I was shocked and didn't see it coming, because I thought that Ava was doing it out of depression, a desire for attention, and anxiety about her future, or was there also an underlying thread of prejudice against trans people? I'd like to think it was all the former, but I can't be 100 percent certain.

Shortly after my birthday, my friend Katie, in whom I had confided, sent me a book she had just read. Katie has supported everything I've done for years. She was one of the first to encourage me to write and blog, and every so often she said, "One day, when you write your book…" She's also one of the most avid readers I know and the person I always turn to for book suggestions. She sent me the novel *This Is How It Always Is* by Laurie Frankel. It's about a trans girl and her family, the difficult decisions the parents have to make regarding their child, and how having a trans child affects the whole family. Although it is fiction, the author has a trans daughter and draws from her own experience.

I remember reading the book in three days and enjoying it but feeling frustrated because the main character wants to wear dresses starting as a toddler. I hadn't come across any reading that was about kids who don't present as trans until their teens. The part I identified with the most was the afterword. The author wrote, "No matter the issue, parenting always involves this balance between what you know, what you guess, what you fear, and what you imagine. You're never certain, even (maybe especially) about the big deals, the huge, important ones with all the ramifications and repercussions. But alas, no one can make these decisions, or deal with their consequences, but you."*

---

* Laurie Frankel, *This Is How It Always Is* (New York, NY: Flatiron Books, 2017), 326.

CHAPTER 4

PUSH *and* PULL

Air, air, I need air, help. I made it to the other side of the crosswalk before stopping my run to put my head down and hold it between my hands, trying to increase the blood circulation to my head to stop the dizziness. I watched the sweat from my hair drip onto the concrete sidewalk as I tried to take deep, calming breaths. My runs were my only time to process and try to accept what was happening, but in the past few weeks, I had been alternating between panic attacks and crying spells while running, as Ava kept pushing the boundaries.

The day before, on August 4, I had walked into her bedroom and frozen at the sight of her little black chalkboard. In the center, she had written in large capital letters, "I AM STRONG." On one side, she had drawn a striped flag and written "bi pride" beneath it. Later I learned that this was the bi pride flag — pink on top, lavender/purple in the middle, and blue at the bottom, the purple representing the overlap between the colors and attraction to both sexes. On the other side, she had drawn the transgender symbol and written "MTF" (male to female) under it. This was in plain view in her room. I didn't think that Shayda would really notice or ask about it, but surely Armon would notice it any minute, and we still hadn't told Ava's siblings what was going on.

Under her desk, I had noticed piles of her old toys and books, stacks of Pokémon cards and Super Mario video games, and an overflowing bin of Legos. In her lonely years, she had spent hours in her bedroom building the most complicated things out of those plastic bricks. The only toys of Shayda's that Ava had ever played with were the Lego Girl sets — Lego dollhouses and Lego kitchens. Ava had never shown an interest in Shayda's Barbies. Even if she had, it would have reminded me of my own childhood of playing with Barbies and GI Joes with my cousin, and I would not have cared. Again, I recalled that she never gravitated toward Shayda's other toys or princess costumes.

But what is the difference between a girl toy and a boy toy? I don't know. Years ago I saw a diagram on someone's Facebook page that I shared on my wall. It was called "How to Tell If a Toy Is for a Boy or a Girl." It said that if you operate the toy with your penis or vagina, it is not for children. If you don't operate the toy with your genitals, it is for both. I agreed, but I also knew that when I was a kid, all I wanted to play with were dolls and Barbies and Fisher-Price figures and houses. All I ever wanted to play was "family." And I always got my cousin Farshad to play whatever I was playing.

On top of Ava's desk I caught sight of a book titled *If I Was Your Girl*, with a trans girl on the cover — a young adult novel she had checked out from the library. Every time I walked into her room, the book seemed to be in the exact same spot, making me question whether she was even reading it. I wondered if Hope had suggested that she check out the book and start leaving hints around her room that her siblings could see.

At this time, I was communicating with both my sisters simultaneously via Facebook Messenger. My younger sister Parimah lives in New York City, and my older sister Parastou lives in Cairo. We see each other every summer, and in between, we fill each other in on everything. Early in the morning LA time was a convenient time for all three of us to be online. They were both unsure what to say about Ava, simultaneously supportive yet in disbelief that she could possibly be trans.

I still had not told my parents. I wasn't sure they would be able to handle the news, and I was also afraid my mom would somehow blame it on me, maybe saying that I had spent so much time in the last few years running and doing yoga and writing my blog that I hadn't given enough time and attention to my kids, and Ava's declaration of being trans was indeed just a desperate cry for attention. Or maybe my mom would say that Ava was doing this because I had too many gay friends, so that my child would identify as gay in order to gain my love and attention. I wasn't sure whether my mom understood the difference between being gay and being transgender, between who you are attracted to and who you actually are.

Since I wasn't confiding in my mom, we were drifting apart. I couldn't call her without telling her everything. Parimah encouraged me to talk to her. When I was in Thailand, Parimah told me, my mom had kept pressing her about what could possibly make Ava want to hurt herself, and Parimah had said that Ava was having some questions about being gay. "Mom handled the 'possibly being gay' very well. She didn't care. I think you should tell her what you are going through."

Nervously, I called my mom, my heart racing while I listened to the ringtone. We started with a little small talk that went nowhere. "Is everything okay?" she finally asked. If I was going to tell her, now was the time.

"Everything is not okay, Mom. It's been a hard few months."

"Tell me," she implored.

"It's Aydin. I'm having problems with him."

"I know," she said. "It's okay. I took him for a walk while you were in Thailand and said to him that we all loved him and everything would be okay. Parimah told me that he thinks he is bisexual or gay."

"That's not it, Mom. I wish that was it. He thinks he is a girl."

I don't know that she fully understood what I was telling her, but within a few seconds she said, "It's okay. Everything will be fine. I'm glad you're telling me. Everything is going to be okay."

I went into more details. "He says he is a girl. He wants to wear girl clothes and start taking hormones." I wanted to make sure she understood exactly what I was saying, keeping the language simple but clear. The rest of our conversation is a blur in my memory, with me crying and her reassuring me. Never once did she say anything like "How could you guys let this happen?" I don't know why I had thought she would blame me. Maybe because she often did seem a little critical of the time I was taking away from my kids to run, go on yoga retreats, or spend time with girlfriends. Maybe because I was feeling guilty about the time I had taken in the past few years to try to find my own identity — myself — again. But my mom pointed no fingers. She kept expressing concern about me and Babak.

"You guys need to take care of yourselves. These things can be stressful for couples. You guys don't argue or disagree over him. Do what you need to take care of yourself. Try not to let this affect you at work." I don't think she knew then that this would be real or permanent. I think that, like me, she prayed and hoped that it was some temporary teenage confusion Ava was going through.

I talked to my dad shortly afterward. He had definitely been listening in the background when I was telling my mom, because I could hear him asking her what was going on. When I did talk to him, he said we all needed to come together and support Ava through this time. "This is the situation, and there is nothing we can do but support him."

Once I had told my parents this secret, a huge weight was lifted off my shoulders. If I could tell them, if they knew, then nothing else mattered. No one else's reaction mattered. I'd be okay.

Their reaction to the news was a sharp contrast to mine when Ava told me. I expected my mother's reaction to be like mine — "This can't be true, and it can't be happening" — but it wasn't. They didn't deny the possibility of Ava's being a girl. They didn't say, "This is obviously a mistake that needs to be sorted through and fixed." They said, "We're here for you through this." And with their words, I felt the greatest sense of relief I had ever experienced. I felt like I could suddenly breathe again. But I hadn't been able to give Ava the gift my parents gave me. I didn't give her the opportunity to breathe.

During that phone call, my mom recounted what it had been like for her to look after Ava until Babak and I got back from Thailand. "I was so scared, I didn't know what to do. I couldn't imagine what could be so bad that he was hurting himself. I was scared for him to be alone in his bedroom, so I kept finding excuses to check on him. I'd cut up an apple and take it to his room. Dad and I didn't sleep at all until you got back." That was when she had told me she wasn't sure she would be comfortable watching the kids again. What if something happened while I was gone? How would she live with herself?

Maybe that's why my parents responded with empathy when I finally told them, "He thinks he is a girl." They knew the gravity of the situation from their few days' experience. Something bad had happened on their brief shift of caring for Ava; imagine what could happen on mine.

On August 20, Shayda, Ava, and I participated in the Glitter Run, a five-kilometer run to benefit the Los Angeles LGBT center. I had signed us up for the run in July, thinking it would be a fun activity for all of us, combining running with lots of glitter stations. Shayda and I were waiting downstairs for Ava so we could go pick up my friend Carmelo, who was joining us. Carmelo had been on the Thailand yoga retreat. We had met at dinner on the first night of another of Jake's yoga retreats a couple of years earlier. That night, Carmelo had announced, "I'm your new gay best friend and your kids' new guncle."

I laughed. "You haven't even met my husband or kids."

"Don't worry," Carmelo said, "we're going to all get along and be one big happy family." He was right.

Ava came down the stairs, wearing eyeliner and blush. I didn't say anything. After all, everyone at that run, irrespective of gender, would be wearing makeup and glitter. That was the whole point. When Carmelo got into the car, he said hi to the kids and then looked at me, and we exchanged a knowing smile. Ava had asked me to apply three colors of glitter on her cheeks in a stripe pattern, pink on top, purple in the middle, and blue on the bottom. Despite having seen the bi pride flag on her chalkboard, I didn't pick up on the meaning.

Ava, Paria, and Shayda participating in the Glitter Run,
August 2017; Ava has the bi pride flag on her cheek.

Ava had a great time at that run, looking around at all the gay men
covered in glitter, wearing tutus and wigs. Once again, I was hoping that
this event would show her that she could just be a gay male who sometimes had fun with clothes and makeup. I thought, *Oh, this is so good for
him, to see these men just embracing being themselves and having fun*, but
I was deluding myself. After the run, she told me, "You know Mom, this
is the bi pride flag you put on my face."

"I didn't know that, but that's okay," I responded.

Before we went out for a family dinner that evening, Ava showered,
but then reapplied blush on her cheeks. "What's wrong with your cheeks?"
Shayda asked her.

Armon looked over at Ava and shrugged, "He's wearing makeup. He's
wearing blush."

"No, I'm not," Ava answered.

"You are wearing blush," I said. "They can see it, and so can I, so you can't say that you are not." I was trying to make her uncomfortable and to get her to own up to what she was doing in front of her siblings. But she didn't answer. She left the blush on, and we went to dinner, another boundary pushed through.

Ava had been buying makeup on her own and hiding it in her bathroom. I saw this as more defiance from the child who didn't do anything without my permission. After she wore the blush that day, I rummaged through her bathroom drawers. In the bottom drawer, I found what I expected: a CVS bag with pink nail polish, pink lipstick, and pink blush. In all the times I had read Shayda the book *Pinkalicious*, had Ava ever shown any interest? I wondered what had been going through her mind when she bought the makeup in CVS. Was she scared, nervous, or excited? Did the sales clerk say anything or stare at what looked like a teenage boy buying makeup? Maybe they thought she was buying it for someone else, or maybe they thought, *Kids these days*, or maybe they just didn't think about it at all.

I wondered what type of rush Ava got from buying that makeup. I also wondered whether Rosa, our sitter and housekeeper, ever rummaged through that drawer and saw the bag of makeup while cleaning the bathroom Ava and Armon shared, but then I realized it didn't matter. Rosa had already seen her wearing nail polish and blush.

Ava had just started ninth grade, her first year of high school. She was going to school wearing her gender-neutral clothing with polished nails. On most days she wore some blush and maybe a little eyeliner, too. Thinking back to my own first days of high school, I could barely remember anything from my first two years, other than trying to walk around unnoticed and waiting for 3 p.m. each day so I could go back to the safety of my home. Lunch period was the worst, when I had to try to be invisible for a whole hour, often eating at my locker and walking the halls or killing time in the less-used corner bathrooms. I don't think my parents knew the extent of my loneliness. I asked Ava if she was eating lunch with others, and she said she was, naming a few friends from eighth grade. Looking back, I hope that she considered home a safe space during those months and not the site of a battle between herself and her mom.

My sister Parimah said to me on the phone one day, "Today I was thinking about Aydin wearing blush. I just got a vision of him standing in his bathroom, looking at the mirror, and putting the blush on. I wonder what he thinks and feels as he puts it on. I wonder what he sees in the mirror. I feel so sad. I can't imagine what he is feeling or what he is going through. I can't stop thinking about him or getting that vision out of my head today."

I paused. I realized that I often wasn't thinking about what Ava was going through, but instead what I was going through as her mother. I wasn't having the type of conversations that I should have been having with her. I wondered about my sister's question, but when Ava came home, I didn't talk to her about it.

In September, for her school ID photo, Ava pulled her shirt down over one shoulder, making it look like an off-the-shoulder top, and gave a bigger smile than she had for any other ID photo. For her ninth-grade honors English class, students had to choose a book to write a report on. She chose the memoir *Redefining Realness* by Janet Mock, a TV host and a transgender rights activist. *Great,* I thought. *Now his teacher is going to put together the way he dresses and this book choice, and soon everyone will know.*

Ava was still seeing Hope, but the final straw that made Babak and me decide it was time to say goodbye to Hope was after Ava walked into our bedroom one night.

"I wanted to talk to you guys about something," she started. I patted the bed and asked her to sit beside me. Babak was leaning against the dresser of the bedroom set we'd had for over eighteen years, a solid brown oak set gifted to us by my parents that will probably last us our lifetime together. Ava was hesitant, and we both nodded encouragement for her to tell us what was on her mind. "I was thinking that maybe just in private, you could practice calling me a girl name and use she/her pronouns — just so I can get a feel of what it's like."

I leapt off the bed. I couldn't help myself. It happened without me taking a second to think. "Absolutely not! Why would we do that? How would that work? You haven't even told Armon and Shayda anything yet!" I was furious.

"I know I haven't told them, but you guys could just call me a girl name if I happen to be alone with the two of you, and call me Aydin when they are around."

"How am I supposed to do that? What if I slip up? I'm supposed to look around each time and see if one of them is in earshot before I talk to you? If you are really trans, then you would tell everyone, and everyone would call you by a new name."

She looked defeated. "Okay, never mind. It was just a thought. It's just that I was talking to Hope about how I could feel more…"

Babak interrupted her this time. "If there comes a day and time when we are sure that you are trans and you are ready to tell the world you are trans, then we will call you by a girl name and use female pronouns along with the rest of the world, but until that happens, you're Aydin."

She got up and left the room. I set up an appointment with a new therapist at the end of September, and we scheduled one last session with Hope.

I had asked to talk with Hope myself at this last session. I wanted her to give me her thoughts based on her three months of weekly sessions with Ava. She took me back to her office, this time leaving Ava sitting in the waiting room. We sat across from each other, a mere two feet apart, Hope in her flowy top looking kindly into my eyes, waiting for me to start. "I know that you may not definitely know, but based on your experience and what you guys have talked about in these sessions so far, I want to know whether you think Aydin is transgender or not."

"What does being a girl mean to you?" Hope asked.

"It's who you are on the inside. I'm a woman. I always have been. It's not about makeup or what I wear. You could shave my head and cut off my breasts and I'd still be a woman. It's who I have always been on the inside. I know my child. I've never for once thought he is a girl on the inside. Maybe this is about outside things for him, like hair or clothes or makeup. I don't know. But on the inside, I just don't see him as a girl. I've never for a second suspected it before.

"And we've never tried to put him in a box. When he was a kid, he never tried to put on dresses for us to stop him. When he was eighteen months old, he loved to try on my shoes, and I have a bunch of pictures of him in them. But obviously, I didn't discourage that, because I took pictures and put them in an album. But he wasn't even two. All little kids try on adult shoes. And from what I know, that's before you even have a sense of your gender identity."

A person's gender identity is their personal sense of where they fit on the continuum of male to female. Over the last few weeks, I'd read that most theories on gender identity agree that it is formed in the brain, and that it is not a conscious choice. By age two to three, a child's sense of gender identity emerges; by three to four, they become increasingly aware of the anatomical differences; by four to six, they associate gender with specific behaviors. I had learned nothing about this in medical school or residency. The only thing I learned was that by age three, a child should be able to tell you how old they are, and if they are a boy or a girl.

"I can't tell you if Aydin is definitely transgender," Hope responded. "I can tell you that before I came out as an adult, no one would have ever guessed that I might be trans. I can also tell you that Aydin currently feels and believes he is a girl, and when he is not allowed to express himself as he wants, it causes him to be depressed and think about hurting himself. So right now, I think that the best way to support him is to allow him to explore his gender."

Now when I think back, I'm fairly certain Hope knew that Ava was a girl, but she didn't tell me because she knew I was not ready to hear it. She was telling me what I needed to hear to let Ava explore her gender, keep her safe, and continue to get therapy. She knew that if she said, "Yes, your child is definitely a girl," I would just have come back with "How can you claim to know my child better than I do after three months?" I didn't ask Hope if her parents had ever suspected that she might be trans.

"Well," I said, "I guess we can just let him dress like a girl and wear makeup to school. What's the worst that can happen if we do that and he is not a girl? In a couple of years he changes his mind and goes back to boy clothes, and when he moves on from high school no one will remember or care anyway. Who cares if he had this high school phase where he dressed like a girl and wore makeup? None of that is permanent. So many people completely move on from high school and are not in contact with people from high school anyway. I'm one of those people. I'm completely a different person than I was in high school. And if he is a girl and he continues to want to wear girl clothes and makeup, then we'll just take it as it comes, I guess."

"That's right, Paria. What's the worst that can happen if you just let him wear clothes that make him feel comfortable right now? I have no doubt that you and your husband love him very much and will continue to support him through this. I have other kids that I see who end up leaving therapy, and I worry about them. I'm not going to worry about Aydin leaving and going to another therapist. I have no doubt that you and your husband will continue to support him and that he will be okay."

Damn, she was so nice. I was switching Ava's therapist using the excuses of schoolwork, distance, and convenience, when it was really because I wanted her to go to a "regular," nontrans therapist. Hope must have known, but she still said all the right things to protect Ava. She then gave me a handwritten list that included the numbers for the Children's Hospital Transgender Center and the LA Gender Center for therapy. I took the list and thought, *I'm not calling them. This is exactly what he does not need right now.* I did make a donation to the Colors organization in exchange for the excellent free therapy that Ava had received, mostly to make myself feel less guilty. At the private therapist I'd carefully selected for Ava, I would pay $250 a session out of pocket, but hey, anything to protect my kid.

On a hot and unusually humid day, I parked my car outside the new therapist's home office. It was September 29, 2017, and we were meeting with Anahita, a therapist whom I knew and who was a good friend of my cousin Farshad. She was an excellent therapist, although gender identity and dysphoria were not her field. I asked to have an entire session alone with her before she saw Ava. In addition to making sure she understood that Ava had never had any signs of gender dysphoria before the age of thirteen, I wanted to give Anahita an overview of Ava's childhood through age twelve, conveying my perspective as her mother, as the person who thought she knew her best.

I sat across from Anahita on her couch in her earthy, Santa Fe–esque office. Her fire-red, curly mane framed her face as she looked at me with her amber eyes, and I explained, "I want someone who is going to look at Aydin as a whole person, going back to his childhood. Sexuality and gender are only a part of who he is. There is a bigger picture here that is getting missed."

I took a deep breath and went on, "Aydin has always been a difficult kid. He's been struggling with a place to belong and depression for years. I started getting calls about him from his teachers as early as kindergarten." My lips started to quiver. Anahita handed me a tissue and told me to take my time.

Ava's kindergarten teacher had usually called to tell us things like "He got upset in class, and I can't figure out exactly why. He raised his hand to answer my question, and I picked someone else instead. So Aydin put his head on the desk and refused to participate for the rest of the day." In kindergarten, generally the whole class gets invited to every birthday party. Ava didn't get invited to as many parties as my other two kids. If I did take her to a party and the kids she was comfortable with were playing with other kids, she was always hesitant to join in. I'd have to coax her.

While other moms would arrive at playdates and birthday parties relieved to have their kids run off while they grabbed a glass of wine, I spent the first hour of each party with Ava following me around until I told her firmly that she had to go play with other kids and walked away from her. That type of tough love usually worked.

At first, Babak and I attributed Ava's social difficulties to the fact that she was one of the youngest in her grade. We asked her teacher if she should repeat kindergarten, but she advised against it. "He is so smart and academically ahead of all the other kids, he will be bored to death repeating the year. I wouldn't hold him back."

It was true. Ava was incredibly smart, having more than made up for being a late talker. At her well-child visit at eighteen months, she still wasn't speaking any words, so her pediatrician said it was time to consider speech therapy, but I could tell that she was constantly observing and absorbing the world, on the verge of exploding with words. "Give him until age two," I said to her doctor. Sure enough, just before her second birthday, she took a sip from a juice box and declared, "That's refreshing."

First grade was when Ava's intellect really stumped her teacher. While teaching math, Miss Katz had posed the question, "We can do 1 plus 2, but we can't do 1 minus 2, can we?" and Ava had said, "Yes, you can, it is negative 1." Miss Katz had glossed over this response, not wanting to confuse the other children. Then, when she was asking the kids to give her examples of "en" words like *hen* and *pen*, Ava had said "dentist." She then wanted to continue to give her examples of other "en" words and kept raising her hand.

Miss Katz wanted the other students to have a chance to think of words, so she did not call on Ava, and she got upset. Miss Katz called me about the "dentist" episode, saying that while she didn't have Ava give her more examples, she was curious what other words Ava would have said. This became a recurrent issue: although Ava always knew the answer to the teachers' questions, they limited how much they called on her to give other students a chance. When they didn't call on her, she got upset and sulked, putting her head down on the desk. For years, being the freakishly smart kid was her way of finding a place or identity for herself.

When Ava was about eight years old, Babak's mom got her a big book on ocean life. It was like an encyclopedia. Ava read it over and over, memorizing all the facts in it. It gave her something to do with her lonely time. We thought maybe one day she would be a marine biologist. We followed her lead and took her to the Long Beach aquarium a few times so she could stand in front of the glass and name all the creatures that swam by. She fixated on that book for about six months before moving on.

By this time, I thought that she was probably just somewhere on the autism spectrum, unusually intelligent and socially awkward. On a couple of occasions, I mentioned this to her pediatrician, a colleague of mine, but I said, "There's no point in getting him a formal diagnosis. It's not going to change anything that we are doing for him." We left it at that.

When Ava was ten, there was a new boy in her school, Liam. He was American but had lived in Japan for a couple of years. Ava and Liam clicked immediately, and we were happy to see her develop that type of friendship. Because of Liam, Ava became obsessed with learning Japanese. When I found out that she was teaching herself Japanese online, I bought her the thickest Japanese language workbook I could find. She took it everywhere, working on it even on the ten-minute car ride to school. I drew the line at her taking it out at restaurants. Soon she was reading, writing, and speaking Japanese with enough proficiency that if we had been in Japan on vacation, we'd have been be able to get by. Babak and I talked about trying to plan a family trip to Japan. One day, Ava said to me, "Mom, I'm writing my diary in a combination of Japanese and Spanish, so there is no point in you trying to find and read it."

Unfortunately, Liam's family moved away. After only a year, her first close friend was gone. After Liam left, Ava was deeply lonely again until eighth grade, when she joined musical theater and came out as bisexual. Seventh grade had been her happiest year. "And when he told us he was bisexual, we were completely supportive," I explained to Anahita. "It's not like we are conservative, close-minded parents. We just don't think this is the answer. Now that I think about it, Liam was probably his first crush. And when he came out as bisexual to his friends, initially it got him a lot of attention, and now no one cares, so he's on to the next thing to get him attention. He even trained and ran a half marathon with me last year, and then he completely lost interest in running. This is what he does. Being trans is what's next, although I don't think being bisexual or gay is a phase for him. That part fits."

Anahita nodded, as if taking in all the information I had just spewed out to her. I wondered how she was going to remember the key points without having taken any notes. Her pencil and notepad lay several feet away on her desk.

"The problem with our prior therapist was that she wasn't giving me the feedback I needed or hearing my part. I want to be periodically updated with your thoughts and kept in the loop, without you necessarily having to betray his confidence." I might as well have said, "Basically, I want to be in control of the entire situation."

We scheduled Ava's first session with Anahita for the following week. Ava herself was not upset about switching therapists. She said that as long as she had someone she felt comfortable with, she didn't care who the therapist was, and Anahita is such a warm and welcoming soul that I knew that wouldn't be a problem.

As I was picking up Ava from her first session and we were saying our goodbyes, Anahita said it went really well and to call her the next day so she could give me some insights. That day in my journal, I wrote:

I'm scared to call her. I'm scared she'll say that he may actually be trans. And if she says she thinks he probably is not, then how unhappy and lost is he that he needs to turn to this to get what he thinks he needs. I'm scared of whatever the answer is.

When I called her, she obviously had no definitive answers for me after one session. "Listen, this is what he is going through right now. You said that with his other infatuations like sharks or Japanese, he would lose interest after six months to a year. So for now, you stay present and you let him be. You let him explore his gender and identity. And if a year from now, he still insists he is a girl, then you know it's not a phase like the other things. And if a year from now he's lost interest, then you were there with him for it and let him explore and figure it out on his own. Right now, he needs to explore this. You need to stay in the present and take it day by day and let him do it. Hang tight, mama. Be present."

I don't know what else I expected her to say. She was essentially saying what Hope was saying. "This is who he believes he is today. We can't predict the future, but we need to support him in the present."

That night I talked to Babak. "I guess we will let him be. As long as we don't start anything medical, let's just let him wear what he wants and put on makeup and see where we are in a year."

I decided to open my mind, to take it one day at a time, to not worry about the future. I'd live each day in the present — something I hadn't done in a long time.

CHAPTER 5

DROWNING

My eyes produced record amounts of tears in the fall of 2017. Sometimes the tears were a trickle, other times a steady stream until my eyes ran dry. All I did was cry, almost nonstop. The anger was mostly gone. Denial was not an option anymore. All that was left to do was grieve for a child I felt I was losing.

The Chicago marathon was on October 8, 2017. As one of the six marathons in the Abbott World Marathon Majors, it was a bucket-list race for me. I had entered the lottery to run it the previous year. To prepare, I was supposed to start increasing my weekly mileage and long runs in June, when I got back from Thailand, but then I had gone through a period of indecision about whether to do it. Although I was still running regularly, those miles were slow and tear-filled. I had avoided the fifteen- to twenty-mile training runs required for marathon training, and I hadn't made up my mind about whether I would actually go to Chicago until just a few weeks before. Even a few days before my flight, I kept debating whether I should just forget about it. Why travel across the country to stay in a hotel by myself for three days and run a marathon when all I wanted to do was stay home and cling to my children, particularly the one who seemed to be slipping through my fingers? The last time I had left my kids, I'd gotten that life-changing call from school.

To make matters worse, the mass shooting in Las Vegas happened just eight days before the marathon. I was scared to get on a plane by myself and apprehensive about being in a crowd of forty thousand runners. Visions of the Boston marathon bombing and the chaos in Vegas were parading through my mind. Babak couldn't help me decide what to do. "You're the one who has to ultimately decide," he insisted. "I'm going to be here with them, so they will be fine. You're trying to get me to make the decision for you, and I'm not going to do that."

He knew me so well. For once, I didn't want to be in control; I wanted someone to tell me what to do. Never in my life had I felt so indecisive or so lost. Running was the one thing that had brought me back to myself over the past five years, the one thing holding me together. To drop out of running Chicago felt like it would be going back to square one and losing myself again. But every time I pictured myself in a Chicago hotel without my kids, the river of tears would start to flow again.

In the end, I decided to go. I chose to hang on to running and to myself, but I vowed it would be the last time I would travel for running. After this, I'd only run local races.

It's hard to describe the drive to run marathons, other than to say that it is so hard, physically and often even more so mentally, that when you finish one, you are left thinking, *If I could endure that, then I can handle any hardship and come out on the other side.* That sense was exactly what I needed to recapture.

Chicago hit a record high temperature on October 8, 2017. The air was already thick at 6:45 a.m., when I left my hotel room with butterflies in my stomach. Getting swallowed by the mobs of runners heading to the start corrals gave me a sense of calm rather than panic. Strangely, now I didn't feel scared to be among a large crowd that could be targeted — I felt safe. *I love this community. I love these people. I need to be among them. I am one of them.*

I had a hard and slow race, my body weighed down with grief. I wanted to quit many times. I thought about my kids the entire time. *You left them behind in order to do this. They are tracking you on their phones. You can't let them see you stop and quit. You left them for this....You left them for this.* When my internal dialogue stopped being enough to keep me going, I started talking to myself out loud. "Once you get through this, you never have to do it again." I repeated that mantra over and over until the finish line was finally in sight.

I knew I wasn't going to have a good race, but I had told myself that as long as I finished under five hours, it would be good enough. The mind-body connection is fascinating. I finished in four hours, fifty-five minutes, and twenty seconds, just under the cutoff time I had given my grief-stricken mind and body. I was ready to go home and hug all three of my kids as tight as possible.

When I got back to LA, I wrote my last blog post, called "Farewell." I told my readers that this had been my slowest marathon because my heart was heavy from some critical developmental issues my children were facing that I could not elaborate on, and that I couldn't go on blogging when I couldn't write the entire truth of what was happening. It would be disingenuous. I had an outpouring of supportive comments from my readers, telling me how they had enjoyed seeing me evolve on my running and writing journey but understood that it was time for me to focus on my children.

My blog had been my baby for almost three years. It had allowed me to find and express a whole creative side of myself that I didn't know existed. I had used it to slowly come out to the world about being an immigrant brown kid in the US, to describe how being bullied in the fifth grade was still affecting me as an adult, to explore all my insecurities and my path to trying to rediscover my identity. Although I was saying goodbye to something I had invested enormous energy into over the past three years, I didn't grieve the loss. There was no room to grieve anything but the child I felt I was losing. It was time to come out of denial and focus on that.

Within a couple of months of closing down my blog, I also wrote my last article for *Women's Running*. I had been a regular contributor for two years, writing more than forty pieces that appeared online and three that came out in print. The first time I received a check in the mail for a piece I had written, I was so proud. Although I was paid less for that piece than I made in an hour at my job, it made me feel like a bona fide writer and runner, not just a blogger, further legitimizing my new identity. I thought I could continue to write for the magazine, but I had lost my voice altogether.

For that Halloween, Ava made her own costume for the first time. She dressed as a "progressive 2017 hippie activist" version of Luigi from Super Mario Brothers. She wore Luigi's blue overalls with a green shirt and green baseball cap, but on her shirt, she wrote phrases like "Legalize Kindness," "Speak Out against Bullying," and "Love Yourself." She also wore women's sandals, showing off her candy-apple-red polished toenails. I felt proud of Ava and her costume, in awe of her bravery.

All I ever wanted to do in high school was disappear into the background and draw as little attention to myself as possible. Ava was not afraid. She put herself a little more out there every day. Stares in the hallways and whispers as she passed were not going to stop her. I posted a picture of her in her costume on my Instagram feed with the caption "Progressive Luigi made his own costume this year. 'Legalize kindness.' I'm happy that I didn't have to visit a Halloween store for the first time." I was gradually offering hints of change to people who didn't see Ava regularly. Of course no one ever directly asked questions. They just made supportive comments like "Love the outfit" and "The nail polish is on point."

Despite the pride I felt, I continued to alternate between periods of grief and acute anxiety. One day after we went to my parents' house with my brother-in-law Roozbeh, Ava decided to ride home in Roozbeh's car instead of ours. During the forty-five-minute drive, I suddenly began to panic. What if we got into a fatal car accident, and she was the only one left? Who would take care of her? Would she ever get over it? Would she try to hurt herself? Who would support her through figuring all this out? It was late at night. I kept asking Babak if he was sleepy and needed me to drive the rest of the way. He kept repeating that he was fine. I couldn't wait to get home, and I thought, *I will never have just one of us be in a separate car again.* Even after we got home and Ava arrived a few minutes later, I still worried. All parents worry about their kids' safety, but would a time ever come when she was walking home from somewhere and I wouldn't worry about her being beaten up or bullied?

I've always been a wine lover, and I never worried that I might have a problem with drinking. But during this period, I spent the day waiting for six o'clock, when I was home for the night and could have my glass of red wine. After one glass of wine, I'd start to feel okay, but a second glass would lead me to break down sobbing. At lunch with a girlfriend, when she asked if we should get a bottle of rosé and split it, I said, "Not unless you want me to cry a river into my pasta." We skipped the bottle.

I felt bad for my friends who had to listen to my repeated worries, so I made a point of not mentioning Ava at all during some of our time together. Then I'd get home and pour myself the second glass that I'd skipped at the restaurant and unleash the feelings I'd held in for the past two hours. For the first time in my life, I started to worry about getting dependent on alcohol, and I imposed a "sober Mondays" rule on myself.

One night I was in bed alone, trying to fall asleep but failing miserably. It was a Monday night, and Babak was in Saudi Arabia. This was a new work venture. Every two to three months, he traveled to Saudi Arabia for a week as a rotating surgeon in a new plastic-surgery facility. He had left on his second trip two days before. When he called me, I didn't feel like engaging in conversation. I would give one-word answers to his questions, hoping the call would end sooner. I wouldn't really speak or engage. Finally I said, "I just wish I could fall asleep and not wake up. I don't want to kill myself. I'm not saying I'm suicidal. I'm just so tired...so tired. I just can't do this." I ended the phone call, too tired to talk.

After I closed my eyes to try to fall asleep, I realized that what I had just said to Babak was very similar to something Ava had said in second grade. When I'd first received a call at work from her second-grade teacher, I had thought it would be the same as all the other school phone calls: something had happened in class, and she had sulked and refused to participate for the rest of the class period. But this time, it was different.

"He told me, 'I wish that when I go to bed, my eyes won't open in the morning,'" her teacher said. The teacher tried to press more to understand what exactly she meant, and Ava had said that she just wished that she would never wake up. The teacher was rightly alarmed, but I wasn't as alarmed as I should have been. Maybe because I was so tired at that point — tired of phone calls from school about a child with a stable, loving family and no stress so often being unhappy for no reason, tired of all the extra time and energy I always had to spend on her, tired of knowing that this call meant I'd have to find a way to fit therapy into our schedule, and knowing that therapy would reveal no basis for her unhappiness. Was her statement really that much of a departure from her baseline mood? Or was it just another attempt to get attention?

I had signed forms arranging for Ava to meet the school psychologist weekly. After about four or five sessions, Ms. Garcia came up with nothing. Ava just seemed to want to talk about herself. There were other students with acute problems who needed Ms. Garcia's attention more. We concluded that Ava just wanted one-on-one attention. As a working mother of three, I was already doing my best to give her that, but I'd try harder. I'd carve out more time.

I told both my sisters via email about Ava's wishing she wouldn't wake up. I had actually forgotten about it until my sister Parimah reminded me after Ava came out. Now, as I lay in bed comparing her statement to mine, the magnitude and gravity of what she had said that day finally hit me. At that moment, I heard the front door open.

Armon had just come home after being out with friends. He called, "Goodnight, Mom." I replied with a simple "Goodnight." Being a sensitive and intuitive kid, he could tell just from my voice — from just this one word — that something was not right. He walked into my bedroom and climbed onto the bed and asked, "What's wrong, Mom?"

"Nothing honey, everything is fine."

"Mom, something is wrong, and I'm not leaving this room until you tell me what it is."

I didn't say anything.

Realizing I wasn't going to tell him, and knowing the probable cause of all my stress, he curled his body around mine and held me. "Mom, it's going to be fine. You don't need to worry. Everything is going to be fine." Neither one of us said what the issue actually was, but we both knew. And then my tears slowly started trickling again, this time because I had this incredible teenage son who, just from hearing my voice when I said good-night, had realized what he needed to do. He held me for about fifteen minutes, until I told him that it was late and we both needed to sleep.

The next day, when I got home from work, Babak was standing in the kitchen. He had taken the first flight home, canceling his week of sur-geries in Saudi Arabia and telling the director that he would not be back. Through more than twenty years of ups and downs together — living in four different cities, coping with medical school, residency, multiple jobs for each of us, and having three kids in under five years whom I often felt I was raising by myself — he had never heard me say, "I just can't do this." He vowed not to take any extended work trips again until all three kids were in college.

Shortly after his return, Ava turned fourteen. We had tickets to *Ham-ilton*, which I had bought months before so that all five of us could see it on her birthday. We were all looking forward to it, Ava especially, because she would get to see a live performance of all those songs she'd memorized. Ava wanted to wear a dress — a very simple maroon H&M dress that was not flashy or poufy, but definitely a dress. In the privacy of our bedroom, I warned Babak that Ava was going to wear a dress. "I'm not going to go if she is wearing a dress," he said. "I just want to have a nice day as a family without every person turning to look at us. I'm tired of it." Babak is such a private person. He was not ashamed of her, but he was tired of being stared at everywhere we went. I had to be the one to tell Ava.

"Could you wear something different? Maybe one of the outfits that I bought you and gave you this morning? Those are really cute. They're all from H&M."

"It's my birthday. This is what I want to wear. I bought this for today," she replied.

"Look, Baba doesn't want you to wear a dress. People will be looking at us, and you know how Baba is private and doesn't like attention to him in public. So you're just going to need to wear what I bought you today. Those clothes are gender-neutral anyway. Girls would wear those clothes. I would wear them," I pleaded.

It broke her heart — I could see it on her face. She changed into dark leggings and an oversized sweatshirt-type top that extended below her hips. She had wanted to wear that dress for her birthday. I felt terrible. I told Babak, "We should just let him wear the dress. It's his birthday, and he looks heartbroken. I don't want this day to be ruined for him."

"No," Babak said, frustrated. "I just want one family outing without being stared at. You bought him all those clothes. He'll be fine in those."

We took a couple pictures of Ava and me together before we left, although she didn't want to. "It's your birthday, you have to take pictures on your birthday," I insisted.

Despite the little bit of blush and eyeliner she was wearing, I don't think she has ever looked sadder in any picture. Ava couldn't fake a smile. Her eyes told anyone who saw them that something was going on beneath the surface.

In those pictures, I look old and tired. My makeup is perfect, my smile is there, but, like Ava's, my eyes tell the true story — they show the worry, fatigue, and desperation of a mother trying to hold everything together. I was tired. And I was heartbroken, too.

Once we got to the Pantages Theatre, Ava's mood lifted a little with anticipation and excitement. We took a few more pictures by the

Hamilton signs, and she looks a little happier in those. She was wide-eyed and sitting forward in her seat for the entire magnificent show.

The next day, a Monday, she wore a dress to school for the first time. Until then, she had worn a lot of gender-neutral clothing that 95 percent of boys her age probably would not wear, but not an actual dress. This was another H&M knit dress that she must have bought on her own. It was black, with thin white horizontal stripes, a definite cinch at the waist, and a mild flare to the skirt. It wasn't an oversized T-shirt; it was unmistakably a dress.

That year, Ava started school an hour before Armon, so I dropped her off first and then came back home for Armon. When Ava got out of the car, I saw her as a boy crossing the street in a dress. My heart raced. I was worried about what everyone at school would say when they saw her and how they would react. And I was worried about Armon, who was in junior year at the same school. It would no longer be "Your brother is wearing weird punk-funky, gender-neutral clothes"; it would be "Your brother is wearing a dress."

When I took Armon to school, I said, "I have to tell you something. Aydin wore a dress to school today."

"So, he's been doing that for a couple months," Armon responded.

"No, this time it is actually a dress that looks like a dress. I just want you to know and be prepared if you run into him in the hallway."

He said, "Okay," and seemed unconcerned. A few hours later, he must have run into Ava in the hallway. He texted me, "Mom, you're overreacting. It's not even anything." He amazed me through this whole process. His younger sibling was going to school wearing dresses and makeup without actually telling anyone she was a girl, and Armon was okay with all of it. I think, like Babak and me, he initially thought that Ava was confused, trying to stand out and be different, trying to get attention, but he didn't really care. He wasn't the least bit embarrassed to be in the same school with her. Once I asked him, "Do people ask you why your brother is wearing dresses?"

"Sometimes they'll make comments, like 'What the fuck is your brother wearing?' But I'll just answer them with, 'What the fuck are you wearing? At least he's got some style.' That will usually shut them up." And although people still talked about Ava, who was known in school as "that kid who cross-dresses," no one directly asked Armon about it or said anything to Ava's face.

Later that school year, Armon told me that a girl had said to him, "It's so cool how your parents let you guys be yourself. They're okay with you making rap and your own music. They're okay with how your brother dresses. They must be Democrats." That made me laugh. So her perception was that Republican parents didn't let you be yourself?

The day Ava first wore a dress, I went to a Barry's Boot Camp exercise class in West Hollywood after dropping Armon off. I figured the best way to distract myself was a near-death session of alternating between sprints on the treadmill and weighted squats. My Fitbit would vibrate when I had a phone call, but it didn't show who was calling. I was on the treadmill when my Fitbit vibrated. I immediately thought someone must have said something about the dress, and the school was calling me. *Someone must have beaten him up!*

I didn't know whether to leave class and check my phone. I was arguing and reasoning with myself on the treadmill. *You can't live your life like this. You can't assume every phone call is about him. And if by any chance he is hurt and beaten up and sitting in the school office, then they will take care of him until your class is done and you get there. Parents haven't always had cell phones and been immediately accessible.* I stayed in class, but I was distracted and anxious. Afterward I ran to my locker. The phone call was not from the school.

When I picked Ava up from school that day, she got into the car just like on any other day. Nothing could have happened, because she seemed fine and happy. During this time, I kept waiting for the other shoe to drop, but it didn't. Each time she pushed the envelope, I waited with bated breath. The next day, we had a new normal, and I was okay again.

Then I waited for the next step that she was going to take, knowing it would come, but not knowing when. But there was never a single phone call about Ava's being bullied or beaten up in school.

After that first day in a dress, there was no stopping Ava. She bought women's jeans and women's tops. She wore tops with lace shoulders revealing the skin beneath, and tops with ruffles. As she expressed herself more with her clothing and her hair finally started to grow out, she started wearing less makeup, usually just nail polish and highlighter on her cheeks.

Thanksgiving was less than a week after Ava's birthday. Thanksgiving has always been my favorite holiday. When I was growing up, my family celebrated a very abbreviated Christmas. Sometimes there was a tree, and gifts my little sister Parimah bought from the school store for all of us, even if we didn't always reciprocate. One year she got me a piggy bank made out of an empty one-gallon milk carton. After a few years, when my parents were more settled in Pittsburgh, we had a few inexpensive store-bought presents. We did not celebrate Hanukkah, and I'm fairly sure I never heard about Kwaanza until well into adulthood.

During my childhood years in Tehran, my favorite holiday was Noruz, the Iranian new year, which coincides with the spring equinox. But Noruz is not about presents; it's more about visiting family and friends. Every Noruz, we got a brand-new dressy outfit and shoes that we wore to visit relatives, starting with the oldest. At these visits, the tradition was to hide various small bills, the equivalent of five- to twenty-dollar bills, in the pages of the Quran. Before leaving the relatives' house, we would be presented with the Quran, flip to a random page, and hope that we landed on a page with a larger bill. The more luck you had, and the greater number of people you visited, the more money you collected.

Once we moved to the US, where we had almost no relatives and not many Iranian family friends, Noruz lost its position as my favorite holiday. Christmas became the default American holiday I preferred over Noruz, because even if my family was celebrating an abbreviated version, the excitement of the season, with the lights and the carols, created the same festive atmosphere I had felt around Noruz in Iran. And although even in Iran, before the Islamic Revolution, many people did celebrate or at least acknowledge Christmas as an important holiday as a result of the Shah's influence of bringing more Western culture to Iran, it still didn't feel like *our* holiday. But Thanksgiving was the American holiday we felt we could rightfully celebrate.

My first memorable Thanksgiving was in 1984 at the home of the Richters, the family of my dad's work partner in Pittsburgh, Pennsylvania. If we celebrated Thanksgiving our first year back in the US, when we were living in Madison, I have no recollection of it — like much else from that year, it is somehow erased from my memory. The year at the Richters' was the first time I saw a chocolate pie. I had no idea such a thing existed: I thought all pies were made with apples, cherries, peaches, or some other type of fruit. I was also introduced to a sweet-potato side dish topped with marshmallow that was so sweet it was inedible, even for someone who to this day loves confetti frosting straight out of the can.

That Thanksgiving dinner gave me my first glimpse inside an American family, and it reminded me of what I'd lost when we left Iran. As my older sister engaged in conversation and my younger sister was absorbed with catching glimpses of the Richters' cats as they sneaked under chairs and disappeared, I looked around, the darkest-skinned person in that dining room, committing the details to my memory. There was so much warmth and laughter. Despite the lack of the heaping trays of saffron-colored rice that would have been traditional at any Iranian meal, the table was overflowing with food. As various unfamiliar dishes were passed around, the aroma of turkey and gravy filled the room. The Richters' home seemed to have a golden glow all over it; I'm not sure if that was the lighting or if it's just how I remember it. Their children were so nice, genuinely taking an interest in us with their questions. I didn't feel like anyone had done that in America yet. This was the America I had envisioned when my parents told us we were moving back to the US, not the isolation I'd experienced over the last fifteen months. But despite the warmth I felt, I was unsure when I'd be let into an American family experience like that again.

That was a time in my life when I lived in my imagination, because my imagination was all I had. After that day, I continued to live in my imaginary world, but the scenes in my imagination changed. Why picture myself as a sixth grader with friends who came over for sleepovers or who I went to the mall with? That was never going to happen. Why not imagine my adult life? I was smart. I'd work hard and become a professional. I'd get married and have a lot of kids. Those kids would become adults and come home for holidays, and I'd have my own American Thanksgiving — too much food, people laughing, a warm golden glow, and even the inedible marshmallow–sweet potato side dish. I could and would make this happen.

Once I had my own children, Thanksgiving continued to be my favorite holiday, whether we gathered at my mom's in Pittsburgh, at my house in LA, or again at my mom's when my parents retired and moved to Calabasas. I passed on the love for the holiday to my children. Every year my mom would assign me or Parimah to make the pumpkin pie, never having developed a taste for it herself.

Before Thanksgiving dinner that year, when Ava told me, "Mom, I left something on my bed for you to iron," I knew it would be the maroon dress we hadn't let her wear to the theater. My heart stopped. It wasn't just that Babak would have an issue with it. I worried about my mom. It was one thing for my parents to say they supported us, and another thing to actually see their "grandson" in a dress for the first time. Still, I picked it up, took it to my room, and ironed it, praying furiously while I did it. Then I put it back on her bed, and the arguments and texts started.

I found Babak. "Aydin just told me he left something on his bed for me to iron for today, and it's the maroon dress. I did it. I'm going to let him wear it. I'm not going to be the one to break his heart again."

"I don't want him wearing that for Thanksgiving dinner," he replied.

"Then you tell him. I'm not telling him again. I'm not doing the dirty work again. I don't care if he wears it. If you don't want him to wear it, you tell him."

Ultimately, Babak said nothing about it. When he had to be the one to break Ava's heart and not delegate the task to me, he couldn't do it.

I texted my sister Parimah, who was at my mom's, to say that Ava was coming in a dress and to warn my mom. She called me. "Mom is upset. She doesn't want Aydin to come in a dress."

"I'm not asking for her opinion or permission. I just want her to know so that she won't be shocked when she sees him. I have to prioritize my child's feelings over Mom's feelings right now. It's not easy for me either. I'm not exactly happy about it, and I'm already dealing with Babak on this side."

I also told Babak that we would be taking family pictures that day. For the past several years, our holiday card had been based on a Thanksgiving family photo, and I said that this year would be no different. "I'm not taking family pictures if he's in a dress. We're going to mail out pictures to people across the country who haven't seen him in a long time, and suddenly our son is in a dress?"

"I'm taking our family pictures today, whether you like it or not. I've done it every year, and you can be in the pictures or not. What do you think will be more strange, a holiday card without you in it, or one where our son is wearing a dress? I'm not ashamed of anything that's happening. And if this really is happening, then people are going to know sooner or later, so they may as well not be completely shocked if it happens."

That Thanksgiving dinner was full of tension. I put a big smile on my face, grabbed a glass of wine, and did my best to make it a normal Thanksgiving. We went to the backyard to take our family picture, and Ava was thrilled. For the holiday card, I ended up cropping the picture to show us all from the waist up, so it wasn't obvious that she was in a dress. In the photo, Ava's smile is huge, in contrast to her birthday pictures. The only person whose smile looked a little forced was Babak. Armon and

Shayda were smiling, unaware of any of the behind-the-scenes drama of the day, and unfazed by their sibling in a dress.

Thanksgiving 2017 family photo, with Ava wearing the maroon dress.

The next day I wrote the following journal entry:

My mother looked so tired and sad yesterday. How much of it was because Aydin was in a dress, and how much was the general fatigue of preparing a Thanksgiving meal and having 3 little grandkids with her all week, I don't know. I felt bad...seeing not just the fatigue in both my parents' faces but the lack of joy yesterday, neither looking like they were enjoying themselves. I felt bad — but what can I do....If I was sure this is all fake, I would put my foot down and say Aydin, you're not wearing a dress and deal with it — but I'm not sure anymore. And if it's not fake, I can't have him look back in the future and we were the parents that didn't support him. It's all exhausting, but it is the truth of what's going on now.

I was in a state of constant exhaustion, not just because of my own continuous praying and crying and questioning but also because of worrying about everyone else's feelings. My eye twitched frequently, particularly when I was at work, trying to focus and not let my homelife interfere with giving my attention to other parents and their children. I'd often get to work, find one of my colleagues Nicole or Pam, and sit and cry for a few minutes while I caught them up on what was happening. Then I'd dab my eyes dry, saving my mascara. I'd take a few deep breaths and walk into the first patient room with a big smile. Work was both impossible and my salvation. It was the only time I was forced to shut out everything else from my mind so I could focus on my patients.

The day after Thanksgiving, I found Ava moping around and looking sad. "What's wrong?" I asked.

"I definitely see myself as a girl in the future. I don't see myself as gender-nonconforming or nonbinary."

Over the past few weeks, I had started asking Ava about these possibilities, thinking that if she was nonbinary, it would be easier for her than being a trans girl. She could keep the same name and not start hormones or ever consider surgery — just be. I guess she must have been trying to consider that option, but it made her depressed.

"Saying I'm nonbinary, it's not who I am. I am a girl. To say I'm nonbinary is an omission of who I really am, and an omission is a lie."

I was struck by how powerful that statement was: an omission about who she really was would be a lie.

In a way, it reminded me of when she told us she was bisexual. At the time, I thought she should just commit to saying she was gay rather than trying to ease people into the idea by saying she was bisexual. A few months later, I had asked her about it again, "Do you still feel like you are bisexual and not just gay?"

"Yes, I am bisexual," she maintained.

"What makes you say that? How do you know?"

"When I look at someone, I don't really think, is this person a boy or a girl? I just think this person has really nice eyes, or this person has a great smile, or this person is so kind. I'm attracted to the person as a being, not as a gender."

I thought, *Wow, that is a great explanation. I'm going to stop saying I think he is gay.* I was so impressed that a child of twelve or thirteen would look at people and see them for who they were. And part of me was also proud of myself for raising this kid who just saw people as people. Later, I learned that many trans people are bisexual or pansexual. Because they've had to dissociate their own genitals from their gender, they just look at another person as a whole, regardless of assigned sex, and may be attracted to someone regardless of gender. I thought that was actually quite beautiful — to have a sexual attraction to a person because of who they were, regardless of body parts.

When Ava told me that saying she was nonbinary was an omission of the truth, I had a wake-up call: *This could be real. I need to take this seriously, and I need to stop telling her maybe she is just nonbinary.* And I again found myself proud that this person I had raised was aware of the importance of being herself, of living her truth.

A few months later, when I started attending Transforming Family support group meetings, I came to realize that being nonbinary was a lot more complicated and harder to explain to people than a masculine/feminine binary. If you tell people that someone doesn't identify as boy or girl but as some of both, they say, "Well, if they identify with both genders, then why not just go with the one assigned at birth, rather than both or *they/them*?" But omitting or denying an aspect of someone's gender identity is a lie and not a true acknowledgment of all that they are. Of course, explaining all of this to other people should not be what one cares about, nor should anyone feel the need to explain themselves or their family, but it is definitely harder to explain a nonbinary gender identity and the choice to use *they/them* pronouns rather than *she/her* or *he/him*.

The idea of gender being a spectrum is difficult for a lot of people to understand in the binary world we live in.

As reality started to set in, my emotional state continued to deteriorate. I remember running into another pediatrician, Monica, in the hospital, when I was there to see newborns for our practice. When she asked how I was doing, I started crying and told her everything. I didn't know how to lie and just put a smile on my face and say, "I'm fine," and make small talk. If I let myself stop to think, I cried. I just had to go through the motions of my day. I remember comparing myself to women whose husbands have a double life and who claim they had no clue. I would always criticize those women: *How could you not have any clue? You were in denial.... You were choosing not to see what your husband was doing.... How could you not have any clue that your husband had this whole other life?* During this phase, I realized that maybe it was possible to have no clue. Here I was as a mother and a pediatrician who had not had any clue whatsoever that my child was trans.

I criticized myself as a mother over and over. I kept going back to the thought that all I had ever wanted to be was a mother, that motherhood was 90 percent of my identity — and I was a terrible mother. How could I not have known? I had always sensed something was off with Ava. I was always afraid of finding out she had been bullied or abused or of discovering something else to explain her sadness, her loneliness, and her difficulty making friends, but I never had an inkling that the something could be this. I had considered the possibility of her being gay, but never the possibility of her being trans. I didn't know the signs.

The gender of my kids was a part of my identity. Whenever parents at work asked me about my kids, I described myself as a "mom of two boys and a girl." When I met parents who had two boys and were pregnant with their third child, I told them how I didn't think I'd ever have a girl, and I did. It was a part of my story, a part of my history. What was my identity now? A mom of a boy and a girl and a possible trans girl? A mom of two girls and a boy? How long would it take for me to go from saying, "I have two daughters and one son" to actually believing it, to feeling it in my core, to making it my new true identity? Would I ever get there?

In the midst of all of this, we had to find a new therapist. By late October we'd had to end the therapy sessions with Anahita because she was changing her work schedule and no longer doing standard therapy sessions. Searching for therapist number three, eventually, I found Jane Lancaster. Her website said she had LGBT and transgender experience. We set up a first appointment for November 30. Ava had been without therapy for about a month, and I was eager for her to have someone to talk to again. I reflected that maybe I had given Anahita too much information up front, too much of Ava's history of temporarily clinging to different interests before moving on and what I saw as her desperate need for attention. Maybe I had tried to control the therapy sessions too much. Maybe this time I should just step back and allow Jane and Ava to figure it out. Maybe I needed to surrender control and let it be.

Our first appointment was supposed to be a standard fifty-minute therapy session. Jane looked to be in her mid-fifties, dressed in a pant-suit, with perfect makeup and not a single flyaway hair. She reminded me a little of Hillary Clinton. Although her appearance was a contrast to Anahita's easy look of Converse sneakers, jeans, and wild red hair, she had a warm expression while simultaneously looking perfectly composed. I left Ava in her hands and was once again sitting in the waiting room, heart pounding, checking my watch every few minutes, and wondering what they were talking about. After twenty-five minutes, Jane came to the waiting room and asked me to join them.

"I really don't think I'm going to be the right therapist for your child. I think that you need to call the Los Angeles Gender Center and take

Aydin there. I would be doing you a disservice if I told you that I can provide the appropriate guidance." She handed me a piece of paper with the number for the LA Gender Center and the Children's Hospital Transgender Center, just as Hope had done.

I was furious inside. I did not want to go there. What had Ava told her in just twenty-five minutes to make Jane decide that she was not comfortable treating her? Now, with the holidays approaching, it would probably be January at the earliest before I could find Ava a new therapist.

In the car ride home, I was driving with my hands clenching the steering wheel. "I'm sorry, Mom." Ava was looking at my face while I stared straight ahead.

"It's fine. It's not your fault," I replied in a monotone voice.

"But you're clearly upset, and I'm sorry it didn't work out with her. She seemed nice. She just didn't seem comfortable with me."

"It wasn't you. It was her. And I'm not upset at you. I'm angry that I spoke with her on the phone a few weeks ago explaining everything and she said she had experience with this, and now we've wasted our time and lost more time. But it's okay. We'll find someone. We'll figure it out."

I felt defeated and hopeless. I wanted to cancel our upcoming holiday ugly-sweater party. I wanted to take a leave of absence from work. I wanted to just shut down. I went to the fridge and ate two slices of pecan pie, knowing that I was trying to eat my emotions. I watched some mindless TV and fell asleep on the couch. Ava could tell that I was frustrated, that I was shutting down. She kept giving me hugs, saying everything was going to be okay, trying to comfort me and get me to make eye contact and talk to her. I realized that I couldn't shut down. She couldn't see me like this. She shouldn't have to be the one comforting me. I'd start over in December. I knew I should probably find a therapist for myself as well, but I didn't know how I would find the time. The thought of investing the time in therapy for myself seemed to cause me more stress.

My journal entries from December are all over the place. The constant theme is "I'm going to start over with a positive attitude tomorrow," followed by an entry the next day when I'm crying and feel I've failed again. I am breaking down and coming apart. One day in my journal, I ask myself why, when people see me and ask how the kids are doing, I can't just answer with a simple "They are well." I write that saying they are well feels like a lie, and I don't lie. I'm a truth teller.

I'm reminded of Ava saying an omission is a lie, and I wonder if Ava has felt like her whole life is a lie. I decide I'll start writing again. I miss writing and my blog, and so I'll start writing privately to find a way back to myself. I start to write a piece called "Iron," which I share with Babak and just a few other people. I don't know then that part of "Iron" will become the prologue for a book.

December culminates with another call from a school counselor. She wants me to know that Ava walked into her office the week before and told her that she was having some suicidal ideations, although she had no plan and didn't think that she would actually hurt herself. The counselor had been meeting with Ava weekly for a while, which was news to me. I explain to her that we have been in between therapists, and so it has been a more difficult time for Ava, and I'm glad the counselor has been there for her. I get worried that my whole life, I'm going to be waiting on edge for the next phone call like this. I wonder if Ava will ever be happy for more than a few hours or a few days at a time, or if I'll have to spend my whole life worrying that one day she'll hurt herself, or finding out that she did. I don't want to live in the belief that one day that horrible phone call will come. I don't want to give up on Ava's being happy one day. I will not give up on it. My options are to either figure this out or know that the dreaded phone call will be in my future. I choose figuring it out. I choose my child.

CHAPTER 6

CROSSING BRIDGES

On a beautiful December day, I was walking across the bridge from the parking lot into Target, looking at the people entering and leaving the store. Twelve years into living in Los Angeles, I'd gotten used to Christmas decorations and the aroma of gingerbread lattes in the air co-existing with sunshine and people wearing shorts and tank tops. *I wonder what is going on in their lives?* I thought. I no longer looked at anyone the same way.

Just as I was about to grab a shopping cart, my cell phone rang. I looked down at a number I didn't recognize. By now I was used to answering every unrecognized call rather than letting it go to voicemail, but I always felt a little nervous at the sight of a new number.

"Hi, is this Paria?" said a sweet woman's voice. It was Stacie, one of the founding parents from Transforming Family, the support group for families of trans individuals. We had heard of this group through Babak's work: when he first started doing some transgender top surgery, he donated a small amount of money to them. I had finally emailed them about attending a meeting. Their meeting times and locations are kept secret for protection. After you contact the group through their website, an administrator contacts and screens you by phone, and they send you the location of the next meeting.

I poured out our story to Stacie, saying repeatedly that this was all so new. It was still only about six months since we had first found out, although my old life seemed lifetimes away. I was trying to convince her that I couldn't possibly have a trans kid while simultaneously telling her that I needed to start attending their meetings. She was kind and patient. "My daughter presented by the time she was five, and at that time, I was desperate to find other families going through the same thing."

I found myself frustrated again. I didn't want to go to a meeting with people whose children had all presented when they were really young. I needed to hear a story like my own. But Stacie was so sweet and reassuring, so nonjudgmental, so empathetic. She gave me the information for the upcoming meeting, just a few days away.

I'll never forget my first Transforming Family meeting. I really did not want to go, but I felt like I had no choice. Babak had even less desire than I did to attend — he's not a sharer or support group type of person — but he knew I'd need the emotional support, so he decided to accompany me. We walked into a big reception area full of parents, little kids, teens, and young adults. The diversity of Los Angeles was reflected in the diversity of families there. I looked around for some sort of authority figure, found a man with a clipboard, and walked up to him. He smiled. "This must be your first meeting. You're in the right place. In a few minutes, we'll get divided into different groups and rooms."

I looked around at all the people, glad I had decided not to bring Ava with me or even tell her where we were going. I wanted to check out the group for myself first. Having her there in addition to everything else that was new would have been overwhelming. It's the type of scenario you never imagine yourself being in as a parent.

Until a few years before, I hadn't even known that there was a support group for trans families. Never in a million years had I ever imagined that we would be a part of one. Looking around at the parents, I kept wondering, *What are these people going through? Why am I among them? I don't know if I should be here. What the fuck am I doing here?*

We divided into groups: parents of teens, parents of younger kids, the teens, the kids, the siblings. The parents of teens and older individuals were divided into two groups because there were so many of us. Even so, there were at least forty people in our subgroup. It was moderated by a parent and one of the Los Angeles Gender Center therapists, Mark Samuelson. Mark was transgender.

First the parent moderator read a statement: "Transforming Family is a safe space to express ourselves. We are all at different stages of this journey and here to give each other support, not judge anyone on where they are in the process. Please remember that anything said here and all the attendees are to remain confidential." Then we went around the room introducing ourselves briefly, saying if it was our first time attending the group, and letting the moderator know if we had a pressing question we wanted him to circle back to after the introductions. Some parents were there by themselves, others with a partner. Some had brought a friend or one of the child's grandparents.

Then it was my turn. "My name is Paria. Our son told us about six months ago that he is a girl. He came out at thirteen, and there have never been any signs that he might be a girl, so it has been a complete shock, and we're not sure if it is true or a phase." My tears had started within a few words of opening my mouth, my voice was shaking.

Almost all of the other parents were talking about their children using their "preferred" names and pronouns, not the birth or "dead" ones (a term we learned about and didn't like). I justified, "We are still using his birth name and pronoun because he is still not out to other people anyway."

The parent moderator said, "But your child is out to you."

I felt hurt by his statement. It felt judgy, despite the opening statement acknowledging that we were all at different stages on this journey and not there to judge others. For the rest of the meeting, the parent moderator and the therapist referred to Ava as "she," which was hard for me to hear. I winced internally every time I heard it. The other parents mostly tried to refer to Ava as our child and use gender-neutral terms. It was hard.

At that meeting, information came at me faster than I could absorb it. Issues and questions ranged from "My child just came out" to "My son asked for an STP for Christmas — where is the best place to buy one?" An STP ("stand to pee") is a device used by transgender men that allows them to void standing up.

I heard the stories of multiple other parents whose kids did not present until they were twelve or older, and these looked like "normal," concerned, involved parents who, like me, felt they knew their children. That was comforting in that we realized we were not the only ones to get hit with this out of the blue, not the only ones who had no idea and whose kid had shown absolutely no signs as a toddler. But it was horrifying to grasp that if other parents were recounting similar experiences, then maybe this was real, maybe it wasn't a phase. That possibility was a lot to handle.

We learned from Mark that kids who present as trans when they are older have often been thinking about it for months or years, researching and watching YouTube videos and gathering and processing information, so that by the time they tell their parents, they are ready to finally tell other people as well and start to transition. They have spent a long time doing what he called "coming in" and being sure of who they are before "coming out." For the parents, the decision seems to come completely out of the blue, but for the child, it is the result of a long process. That aligned with what Ava first told us when we came home from Thailand and she gave us an entire dissertation on being trans. She had been researching for a long time. For us, it was new; for her, it was not.

I spent all of that two-hour meeting soaking up information, with tears streaming down my face, crying because I was finally hearing stories that resonated with me, terrified of what was to come, and feeling sad and guilty over the six months that I had been denying what my child had been telling me.

At the end of the meeting, Mark urged us to get Ava into the Children's Hospital of Los Angeles (CHLA) transgender center and start her on hormone blockers, at least. "Well, even though he is only fourteen, he is already Tanner 4, so he is beyond hormone blockers," I said. The Tanner scale, also known as the sexual maturity rating or SMR scale, is a measure of physical sexual development: it has five stages, with Tanner 1 being prepuberty, Tanner 2 being the start of puberty, and Tanner 5 being the completion of puberty. The optimal time to go on hormone blockers is at Tanner 2. Hormone blockers, or puberty blockers, inhibit the development of secondary biological sex characteristics, such as breasts and facial hair.

"Hormone blockers can still do a lot for your child."

I just felt like he didn't know what he was talking about. *He's a therapist*, I thought, *not an MD. Our child is almost done with puberty, so what are blockers going to do for him?*

What struck Babak the most from that meeting was the advice from Mark: "Don't be your child's first bully," and "No child ever says, 'I wish my parents hadn't supported me through that confusing time for me.'"

Had we been her first bullies?

I immediately recalled the incident when Ava had walked into our room, asking if we would call her by a girl name in private, and we had said no. I wanted to throw up. After years of begging my child to tell me what was causing her sadness, I had been unwilling to listen. I had invalidated her over and over. We hadn't supported her appropriately for the preceding six months.

I left the meeting completely drained, knowing that it was time to listen to what Hope had told me months before and what Jane had told me after just one brief meeting with her. It was time to find her a therapist through the LA Gender Center and stop denying my child what she needed.

By December, it had been six months since Ava had gotten a haircut, as she had refused to cut her hair since coming out to us in May. Her mop of faded pink was all over the place. I convinced her that a trim and shaping it would make it look and grow in better, that we were not going to shorten it. Babak's cousin Sahar was visiting for the weekend. Before she arrived, I had warned her that Ava was going through this gender confusion and questioning. I hadn't had any worries about her being supportive. Accompanied by Sahar, we went to see our stylist, Matthew, to get both Armon and Ava a haircut.

Matthew had been cutting Babak's, Armon's, and Ava's hair for a few years now. Babak had already explained to Matthew why Ava hadn't been there recently. "Every girl knows that to grow out your hair you need to trim it regularly," Matthew had told Babak. Sahar and I sat at a nearby Starbucks while Matthew trimmed Ava's hair, evening out the ends, and then blow-dried it very straight and smooth for her. Armon saw Ava first and texted me to "be prepared."

Sahar and I looked up to see Ava coming down the escalator with a little smile on her face, unable to hide her excitement. Straightening out her hair had made it look longer, more like a girl's haircut. "It looks great. I love it," I said. "You can go get yourself a drink from Starbucks while we wait for Armon to get his haircut."

I handed Ava money, and she disappeared into Starbucks. A few minutes later, she came out still smiling, mocha latte in hand, and sat by us. I noticed that her coffee cup had the name Lucy on it. "Did you give the name Lucy?" I asked.

"Yes," she answered. I didn't say anything. That was the first time I had any clue that she might be using a different name sometimes in private. Sahar just smiled, not remarking on or drawing attention to anything.

When Armon came down and saw the latte, he said, "Why does your cup say Lucy? Why did you give that name?"

"I wanted to."

"It's fine," I said, changing the subject so that Armon would drop it. When we got home, I told Babak about it.

"Lucy? He does not look like a Lucy. I'm not calling my kid Lucy," Babak said somewhat angrily. Rather than actually talk to her about the name, we just ignored it. That was the last we heard of Lucy for a couple of months.

Ava's excitement vanished two days later when she had to wash her hair. She has naturally wavy hair, and without the blow-drying and straightening techniques of a professional hairdresser, it did look shorter after her trim. She was sulking and looking depressed, and it was breaking my heart. I wrote in my journal the next day:

> Yesterday, Aydin was not happy with his hair. I found myself wanting to help my baby be happy — whatever that took — whether it involved making his hair look more like a girl's or not, just making my baby happy. I felt myself seeing him as my child and not boy or girl — felt the instinct of just wanting to do what I can to make my child happy. It was good to feel that. It was a glimmer of hope for one day being happy with whatever the outcome may be.

That was probably the first moment of looking at my child and not seeing boy or girl, and probably the first time that I realized it might be possible to see her as a girl one day. These glimpses made me both happy and sad, bringing up new emotions. They were the first hints of how I would evolve as a mother. Just a few days later, on December 18, 2017, I wrote:

> Last night, I looked at him, and I could see a glimmer of a future girl. His hair and little makeup making it come through, and I thought about how I'd get used to this if I have to.

One day during winter break, I took Shayda and Ava to the mall with my friend Juliet's kids, Mila and Jackson. They went to different schools, but they had been friends since Shayda's birth. I had met Juliet just a few days before Shayda was born, shortly after we had moved to Los Angeles. Juliet was the president of a local mom's group that I had joined in an attempt to make friends in LA. When I first saw her, with her off-the-shoulder white top against her brown skin, and chunky accessories high-lighting her face, I thought to myself, *Oh, we're definitely going to be fast friends.* I had no idea then that she had also grown up as a brown girl in Pennsylvania or that she'd be the first person to tell me, "You have stories to tell, and I think you need to start writing them down."

Jackson and Ava had always been close, and they walked off together through the mall. Ava was wearing a dress, the black one with white stripes that was the first dress she had worn to school. She also had on women's sandals with her toes polished bright red, but she still looked very much like a boy — a teen boy in a girl's dress and shoes. Jackson was in jeans, a sweatshirt, and tennis shoes, looking very much like a young teen boy who just throws on whatever is lying around in his room. These days, any-time I walked in the mall or went anywhere with Ava, most people would give a quick second glance at what seemed to be a boy in girls' clothing. I would try my best to ignore these looks. I wondered how Jackson would feel about walking with Ava in the mall, all eyes on them. Ava was still not out to Jackson: as far as he knew, Ava was still Aydin, cross-dressing for fun. But even if Jackson wasn't completely unfazed by Ava in a dress, he sure acted like it. He didn't seem the least bit uncomfortable walking with her. Sitting at a table in the dining area, I saw Jackson and Ava walking toward me. Ava had a big smile and was carrying an H&M bag, and they were immersed in conversation. I took a picture of them that I've kept on my phone.

I was so impressed with Jackson. *He doesn't care.* I couldn't imagine myself as a teenager in that scenario. All I wanted to do was fit in. I would never have had the guts to be either of them, Ava in her dress or Jackson walking with her.

Juliet and her husband, Jack, came over for dinner that evening. We had pizza delivered, and we drank wine and laughed. I had a reassuring phone conversation with my dad, who told me, "We need to all be supportive and take this day by day." I felt happy for the first time in a long time. I thought that if I had my few good friends and my family, everything would be okay.

A couple days later, Ava's friend Gavin was supposed to come over. Gavin was in eighth grade, a year behind Ava and not yet attending her high school. They had become very close the prior year in musical theater, but now it had been months since Gavin had seen Ava. While he might have seen her in some gender-neutral clothing, he definitely hadn't seen her in girls' clothes or with her hair grown out. Ava wore skinny jeans with a lacy, feminine black top. She wore sandals that showed her painted toenails and a hint of blush. The two of them were supposed to walk to Beverly Drive and get lunch. I was nervous, worried that Gavin would not want to go out with Ava after seeing her. But that didn't happen. Gavin came over and they sang a little while Gavin played guitar, and then they walked to lunch and back.

What did Gavin think the first time he saw her like that? I don't know. But he certainly didn't make an excuse to not go to lunch. He didn't leave early. They had a good time. I told myself that I just needed to relax. It was all going to be okay. All I was doing was projecting my own insecurities about my terrible and lonely middle school and high school experiences on these kids. I needed to stop that.

My year of being bullied in fifth grade caused lasting insecurity, wiping out my self-worth and shaping my reactions to everything into adulthood. I realized that not only had I been letting that bullied little girl dictate my life as an adult, but I'd also been projecting all of my feelings onto my children, afraid that they would have the same experience. Looking back, I did make a few friends in middle school and high school, and my few girlfriends in Pittsburgh were really sweet and accepting girls. But my own insecurity stopped me from getting too close to them or being comfortable accepting invitations from them. I spent all of my teen years alone, waiting for college, when I could reinvent myself and just start over. And I did, putting on an air of confidence, making new friends. But I also felt the constant need to prove myself and to say, *I'm just like you. I'm like any other American. I'm good enough to be friends with.*

And then 9/11 happened — a huge setback for every brown American, let alone a Muslim like myself, even if I wasn't observant. Babak and I were not fans of any kind of organized religion. But all the devout Muslims I know are among the kindest-hearted people I've met. After 9/11, along with every other brown person in America, I held my breath any time there was news of any type of shooting, praying to the universe that the perpetrator was not brown — or, worse, brown and Muslim.

The election of Donald Trump certainly did not help matters. Trump was publicly denigrating immigrants and people of color and drafting policies on travel bans specifically for people of Iranian descent. And despite finally getting to the point where I knew my own worth, the feelings and memories from my past were still always in the background.

When you've spent your entire life on the outside, that's the last thing you want for your child. It would take me until after I started running and into my early forties to finally realize that I could just stop trying to prove my worth to everyone. Being transgender in the US at this time was the ultimate kind of being on the outside, and I could not help but project my own experiences and fears onto my child. And despite finally getting to the point where I knew my own worth, the memories and feelings from my past were always in the background. When you are a plate that has been shattered and glued back together, the cracks and chips always remain, a permanent reminder of the past.

As I was living through Ava's transition, I was running my fingers over the cracks. It would take a few more months before light would start seeping through my cracks, reminding me of lines by Leonard Cohen, "There is a crack in everything / That's how the light gets in."

On New Year's Eve, I decided to start 2018 with a new attitude. I was going to stop being so afraid all the time, to try to have more hope. It was time to move on. We had a little get-together with just a few friends: Jack and Juliet, Eileen and John, and Carmelo and Kadir. I was not in the mood to see anyone who didn't know everything about our situation or anyone I wasn't completely comfortable with. Ava was wearing a light pink knit H&M dress. (I guess all her first dresses were from H&M, because at this point she was buying her own girl clothes without me, probably scouring the clearance racks for clothes she could afford with any birthday or other gift money she had received.)

At one point, we were all standing around the big kitchen island, with its butcher-block top. Every time we entertain, everyone gathers around the island, and the rest of the house remains unused. Babak was holding his glass of cabernet and said, "Let's go around and all say what the best and worst parts of 2017 have been."

I thought, *Is he fucking kidding, did he just ask everyone to do that?* First of all, that's such an un-Babak thing to do, to ask people to share. Second, did he expect me to answer this question without losing it? I can't remember what everyone said. I know that when it was John and Eileen's turn, Babak joked and tried to get them to say that our trip to Cancun together that summer had been the best part, and when it was his turn, I think Babak said the trip to Cancun was the highlight, but I'm not sure. Did he say what his worst part was? He probably said something about disappointment in something related to soccer or football.

When it came to my turn, I said that the best and worst parts had been the same, and then the floodgates were opened, and tears streamed down my face. Fortunately, all the kids were upstairs and out of earshot. "The worst part has been going through what we are going through with Aydin. The best part has been that it has actually brought Babak and me closer together, having to support each other through it, and also that we've had all of you who have been here from the start and known what is going on and been there for us. Your friendship and presence through this time have been priceless." It was true. My friends had been there for me from the start. I never had to question for a second whether my friends or sisters would accept any of this or be anything less than extremely supportive. After that, I wiped away my tears, and we moved on. It was a lovely New Year's Eve — celebrating with true friends, at home, quiet and simple.

Again that evening, Juliet's son Jackson amazed me. When Jackson came over and saw Ava in her pink dress, he asked no questions. He was unfazed. They went up to Ava's room as they had done in the past, and they played video games or did whatever it is they always do together. They ran around the house with noisemakers, and at midnight, they drank a toast with sparkling apple juice.

That night, once everyone left, I decided I was going to stay up and cry my eyes out and get it all out of my system for 2018. Everyone went up to bed. "I'll be up in a little bit. You go to sleep," I told Babak and headed to the family room couch. I cried for I don't know how long, maybe an hour, maybe two. I bawled and heaved until my eyes were dry, my body exhausted. I waited to see if another wave of tears would come, and when it didn't, I told myself it was time to accept and move on, and I headed up to bed.

Earlier that day, I had posted a picture of myself running on the beach in Thailand on my Instagram feed and written:

> There is no question that 2017 has been the year that the rug was pulled out from under my feet…the year that I've shed a record amount of tears…but it's also the year that showed me that I'm strong enough to find a new rug to walk on…and that if that doesn't work, I'll just figure out a way to fly.…It's the year when there were plenty of occasions for laughter through tears with the people who matter the most…grateful for my husband, parents, sisters, and friends who've been with me through every step of the last year… and for running for being my therapist.

And all of that was true. There were still many tears in 2018, although I'm not sure I had any heaving, break-down-sobbing moments after that

night. Most of the time when I'm in the car alone, I get tearful. I know
there will come a time when I don't. I once commented on something my
friend Jessica had posted about grief never ending, and I said that grief
came in waves for me, that initially I was getting pummeled by waves, but
now, every once in a while, a wave came out of nowhere and just crashed
over me. It's happening less often now, but I suspect that it will always
continue, and I'll never really know or be prepared for what is going to
make a wave.

I started January by taking the kids to San Diego for three days.
Babak had to work, but I wanted to do something with the kids during
their winter break. We drove down and stayed in a hotel in La Jolla, relax-
ing, walking on the beach, and eating out together. In the mornings I woke
up early and went for a run before the kids woke up, then came back and sat
on the balcony, writing in my journal while listening to the waves crashing
on the shore and my kids laughing in the background in my room.

I spent time just observing my three kids, studying the relationships
between them. I saw how Ava still idolized Armon, preferring his company and attention to Shayda's. Sometimes I have to wonder whether the
adoration of her older brother was so great that she would never even allow herself to think that she might be anything that he wasn't. Armon was
always her idol. On Armon's first day of kindergarten, Ava was at home
with me and my mom and newborn Shayda. Ava got so excited when
she saw Armon coming home through the window, realizing that he had
not gone away forever. She kept running around the family room, saying,
"Armon's home, Armon's home, Armon's home!"

A few days after that, she got a cut on her shin that left some dried
blood on her leg. She wouldn't let us wipe it off. She kept saying, "Don't
tell Armon, don't tell Armon." Then we walked to kindergarten to pick
up Armon. As soon as she saw him, she stuck out her leg and said, "Look
Armon, I have blood." She had been waiting for hours to show him.

During open house at Ava's school, I visited her sixth-grade honors English class. On the first page of her poetry book she had written,

"My poetry is dedicated to my brother, Armon. He can get on my nerves sometimes, but guides me through sixth grade well. He is willing to explain a concept I don't understand, and will sometimes play with me. I am thankful that he was born, and it's great to have such a companion." I took a picture of the dedication page and sent it to my sisters. I thought it was sad and sweet, and I remember telling my sisters that Armon didn't just play with Ava "sometimes" but as much as he possibly could when he wasn't doing homework or hanging out with his own friends.

When I look back at old pictures, I see that Ava has a forced, fake smile in so many of them, just like any other kid, but in any picture with Armon next to her, her smile is genuine. Their relationship together has always been special, which is a credit to Armon. He's the kind of person who is deep and feels deeply. Armon has always been in touch with his own emotions and the emotions of others.

Sometimes I wonder if there might have been a part of Ava that subconsciously suppressed her identity because of how much she looked up to Armon. He was her best friend, her everything, still is. Why would you want to not be exactly like your best friend? Why would you even let your brain consider the possibility that you might be in any way different?

Watching them together in San Diego, I let go of the worry that once Ava had told Armon everything, things would change between them. If they were still as close as they had ever been, despite all the changes over the last seven months, then they would probably stay that way. They were still talking to each other nonstop at family dinners and on family walks, sharing inside jokes and laughing about things the rest of the family didn't get. Armon was always patient with her while she talked his head off. He was always her number one outlet for socialization and conversation through all her lonely times, and he was always there to listen to her, although I'm sure it was exhausting for him at times. I felt a sense of peace and calm watching them, realizing that their relationship would probably continue to stay strong no matter what gender Ava ultimately landed on.

Many of the San Diego restaurants we visited had single, all-gender bathrooms. Ava was so much more comfortable going into those to wash her hands before we sat down to eat. It had been a few months since I had started noticing gender-neutral bathrooms, and feeling so grateful for them. These topics in the news were suddenly so relevant, so personal, so important. I grasped the full magnitude of how ridiculous it was to think that women would be threatened by my child using the women's bathroom.

We returned to LA feeling rejuvenated. Every time I was just with my kids, I would realize how lucky I was, how I didn't need anything but these kids being healthy and happy and laughing together. I came back with the renewed hope and perspective I was craving.

On January 7, 2018, I watched the Golden Globe Awards. The "Me Too" movement was at its peak. Women all over were speaking up about sexual harassment, and Oprah Winfrey gave a speech in which she said, "What I know for sure is that speaking your truth is the most powerful tool we all have." She was talking about Me Too, but I knew that I had to start writing the truth again and that one day I'd put it out there, although I had no idea if that day would be in a year, or five, or twenty.

One of the hardest parts of the last year had been the silence I had imposed on myself. Of course, I had told all my close friends and family what we were going through. I shared an occasional family picture on social media showing that Ava was gradually changing, her hair growing out, her clothing feminine, and a hint of makeup on her face. But I wasn't writing, and not everyone knew about Ava because she wasn't out.

I had also stopped socializing with all but my closest friends, because it was hard for me to make small talk and not purge out what had taken over my life. But that ended up being a good thing. I realized I didn't miss that type of superficial socializing. I didn't need to be friends with all these people. Declining invitations that I would normally say yes to was actually good for me. Part of me still felt like the teenager who was an outsider with no friends, and I had been making up for that in adulthood by accepting every invitation that came along. When I was forced to let it go, I was happier. If Ava had the strength to say goodbye to historical gender norms, certainly I could say no to an invite. If I wasn't spending time with a good friend that I could have a real heart-to-heart with, then I preferred to be home with my kids.

Saying no to my close friends was harder. "I can't do a girls' weekend trip right now, I need to be home with my kids," or "I don't think I can do book club for a little while." I was the one who had started our book club twelve years prior. I had to let go of the fear that if I said no to good friends, they might slowly drop out of my life. My FOMO (fear of missing out) was a remnant of my teenage self, and at age forty-four I finally peacefully said goodbye to it.

One day I found myself sitting across from my friend and yoga instructor Jake at lunch, wiping away tears and apologizing for it. He had texted me the day before. "Where have you been? You haven't been coming to yoga or dinner? I never see you anymore." I had explained to him that I was no longer going to do anything on a weeknight unless it was absolutely necessary. Weeknights were for my kids, and weekends for Babak and me to regroup. But if he wanted to meet me for lunch the next day before I went into the office, I could do that. "Sounds great. I'll meet you at Zinqué on Melrose at 12:30. Can't wait to see you," he texted me back.

I placed my order for a quiche Lorraine and salad. Jake just ordered a drink. "You're not eating?" I asked.

"No, I just came from brunch with a friend. I had already made brunch plans before we set this up," he answered.

"Then why did you agree to meet me?"

"Because I wanted to see you, and this was what worked for you," he explained. My tears started rolling down. I was touched that the guru and friend I so admired was willing to go out of his way to get together with me. It confirmed that anyone who couldn't meet me on my terms right now was not a true friend. I filled Jake in on the latest with Ava, telling him we were in between therapists and recounting the call from the school counselor about Ava having suicidal thoughts again. I kept dabbing my eyes with a tissue while talking and trying to eat, and apologizing for crying in front of everyone in the packed restaurant.

"Stop apologizing for crying. I don't care if everyone around us sees you crying. Who cares? And stop beating yourself up for being a bad mother. You are an amazing mother. High school sucks, and so many kids go through terrible periods during high school. Are we supposed to blame all mothers for what their kids go through in high school? You are an amazing mother. Your kids are lucky to have you. It will be okay." Being called an amazing mom despite all the mistakes I knew I had made just made me cry even harder.

On January 11, 2018, Babak said, "We'll cross that bridge when we get to it, unless I jump off it first." I recorded that on my Facebook page with the hashtag "Parenting." I wrote down what he said, but not what made him say it. I know it had to do with Ava, and I'm sure it was in response to my projecting into the future and worrying about some anticipated next step. I loved that while my mind was constantly worrying about what-ifs, Babak was trying his best to take things one day at a time and encouraging me to do the same.

For most of our marriage, I'd felt like I could have done everything without him. Raising the kids on my own would have been harder, but doable. But these last few years, with Armon sometimes experiencing depression and anxiety and then everything with Ava, Babak really stepped up. He was there for them in ways I couldn't be. He came to accept that Ava probably was transgender long before I did. Although he did have a hard time with Ava wearing women's clothes in public while still looking like a boy, his discomfort stemmed from being a private person and disliking public attention. After Thanksgiving, he decided to let go of all of that, and he did. On days when I was falling apart, which was most days, he stepped up as the strong parent.

Maybe most important, Babak was there to support me in figuring out my passions, whether it was running or writing or yoga retreats, so that I didn't keep drowning in all that was going on. He took care of me so that I could take care of the kids. It was a tough few years. I know that a parent's job is to take care of our kids, and I guess all he'd really done was step up to the plate, but not everyone does that. It was especially impressive coming from someone who maintained that without children he would have had a different life, but not necessarily a less fulfilled one.

I wasn't really worried that Babak would jump off the bridge. I knew he would stay and help me cross every bridge we came to. Maybe when the kids were younger the burden had been mostly on me, but those years had been full of things I could handle and things I wanted to control. This, it would have been really hard to handle on my own. For all this, I needed someone to help me cross.

CHAPTER 7

TAKE *the* WHEEL

I had just sat down, waiting for my manicure at Robertson Nails, when I made eye contact with another mother from the high school. It was a typical mid-January day in Los Angeles; 60s weather with the sun shining through the windows. I gave her a smile of recognition — there was no way to avoid it without being rude. I had managed to dodge most of the parents from school so far, not wanting to be asked questions that I didn't know how to answer yet. When she took my smile as an invitation to start a conversation, I assumed it would be about Ava, and not a general question. But she asked, "Do your kids tell you about how everyone is vaping in the bathrooms at Beverly?"

"No," I replied. "They haven't said anything to me."

She pulled out her phone and showed me a Snapchat video her daughter had sent her of the girls' bathroom. About ten girls were standing around, leaning on sinks, vaping and laughing.

"Hmm...this is terrible. The school must know and doesn't do anything about it. I'll ask my kids if the same thing is happening in the boys' bathroom," I said.

When I picked up Ava from school that day, I asked her about it on the car ride home. "I heard everyone is vaping in the girls' bathroom.

Amanda's mom showed me a Snapchat video of it. What about the boys' bathroom?"

"I wouldn't know, I only use the single all-gender bathroom, but everyone is vaping in the stairwells, so I'm sure they are in the boys' bathroom, too."

"You've never been in the boys' bathroom?" I questioned with surprise.

"No," she answered. I don't know why I was so surprised. That's when I found out that she had also been changing for PE class in a private area.

Within three weeks of school starting, Ava walked into the Norman Aid office, the school's counseling center, and asked to speak with someone. She told a counselor that she was a girl and did not feel comfortable changing in the boys' locker room. She requested a private area to change. They arranged for her to change in a locker room used by the dance team, since no one was using that area during the period when Ava had PE class.

Ava was thirteen and a freshman in high school. The courage it must have taken to go and ask for a counselor, tell them she was a girl (when she still looked very much like a boy), and ask for her needs to be met was astonishing to me. That's something that we should have been able to help her with — if we'd only bothered to talk to her more to perceive her level of discomfort, instead of being in denial. That's something parents of other trans kids do for them. Babak and I should have been there to advocate for Ava; she should not have had to do it for herself.

The school also then arranged for her to go to Norman Aid once a week to talk to a volunteer counselor. I believe the counselors were students who were getting their degrees in psychology, who rotated through the high school as interns. On Fridays, instead of going to choir, Ava would go to the counselor. She saw the same counselor once a week for all of her freshman year, while I was switching her from therapist to therapist outside school.

I started to remember all the times when we had gone to a restaurant in the last couple of years and I had made her use the men's restroom.

She always hated using public bathrooms and made the excuse that she didn't need to go. I would insist, "Well, you need to at least go wash your hands." From the age of twelve, at least, she was probably incredibly uncomfortable. The realization about what I had put her through made me feel terrible. Honestly, the men's restroom is probably scary for young kids and teens anyway — all these men standing at urinals rather than using private stalls. If it's uncomfortable for an adult trans person to use public bathrooms, imagine what it's like for a child or a teen. I started to imagine what it was like for my baby.

After that conversation, I went from noticing all-gender bathrooms to looking for them in every restaurant. I'd wash my hands and come back to the table and tell her, "They have an all-gender bathroom, so go ahead and wash your hands." If there was no all-gender bathroom, I stopped making her wash her hands before eating. If I had hand sanitizer on me, great; if not, I didn't bother about it.

Then I recalled Ava's chronic constipation and withholding, which had started around the age of three to four years old and persisted. I started to wonder if part of it had had to do with gender, even though she might not have been aware of the reason. I thought about all the times when she was too old to go into the ladies' room with me and had to go to the men's room by herself, and it broke my heart. I wished that at least for those last couple of years, I hadn't made her use men's bathrooms in public when she didn't have to. Now I'm grateful for every all-gender bathroom I see.

On January 22, 2018, we finally had our first therapy appointment at the Los Angeles Gender Center. A couple of days after filling out intake forms, I received a call from Mark Samuelson, the therapist who had been a mediator at the Transforming Family meeting. He referred us to Dr. Nathaniel Stern, who specialized in transgender teens. Two days a week he saw patients at the Westwood office, fairly close to where we live.

The office was on Westwood Boulevard, right in the middle of a row of Iranian restaurants (and a few Asian ones). To get there, Ava and I had to walk past a number of older Iranians. Although I hate to generalize, they tend to be pretty judgmental and conservative. They all turned their heads and stared openly as we walked past, especially before our initial appointments, when Ava still looked more like a cross-dressing boy. The office was located in an old building behind an Iranian bakery, on the second floor. It had musty carpet and a very small waiting room that offered pamphlets about LGBT support groups, freezing your sperm or eggs, and research studies on transgender people. Again, I had one of those "I can't believe I'm here" moments. We flipped the little switch on the wall that signals to the therapist that someone is there, and waited.

The minute Dr. Stern walked into the waiting room, I liked him. *I'm going to trust him with my kid. We found the right person. I'm going to let him take over.* There was something in his face, his smile, his eyes. Of course I did my immediate quick assessment. *He doesn't look trans. He looks like a cis male, although he has a very comforting, smooth, soothing voice. He is probably gay. He is a little bit of a chubby, teddy-bear gay guy.* Why we make these immediate judgments and assessments about people, I don't know. This is exactly what I don't want people to do to my child. I don't want people to look at Ava and immediately assess her as a trans girl rather than a cis girl. So why was I doing exactly that to Dr. Stern? Maybe because Hope was a trans woman? Even so, I was sure, based on his demeanor, that he was the right therapist for Ava. Maybe I was finally ready to trust someone else with the psychological well-being of my child. Or maybe I was just tired and wanted someone else to take over. For whatever reason, I trusted him right away.

We walked into his office together, and the three of us spoke for a few minutes before I was sent back to the waiting room. For the first time, I was able to actually read a few pages of my book while I waited. I didn't pace the little waiting room with my heart in my throat, ready to be vomited up and spat out onto the floor. I was able to actually think, trying to remember if Ava had ever said anything in her childhood therapy sessions that might have been a clue that she had underlying issues with gender.

Ava was probably in fourth or fifth grade when she and I started going to a family therapist. In the sessions, I would say that I wanted her to try to make more friends or be less lonely. Ava would sit there in therapy, arms crossed, not saying anything. One of the few things she said once was, "I wish that boys and girls could be friends." At that time, Kassidy was the only girl who was friends with her little group of boys. She was active and tomboyish, although she had beautiful long, curly blonde hair, and preferred spending recess with the boys rather than with the girls. "Boys and girls can be friends," either the therapist or I responded. "What do you mean by that?"

"I wish I could invite Kassidy to my birthday sleepover party," Ava responded. I told her that she could invite her, but that since it was a small party with five other boys, Kassidy would be the only girl, and either she might not want to come or her parents might decide they didn't want her to come to a sleepover party with all boys. Ava didn't invite her. That's as far as it went. When we tried to pry more, she crossed her arms again, looked down into her lap, and didn't elaborate.

I don't think she was actually holding something in. I don't think she knew what she was feeling or had the language to articulate it. Kassidy ended up changing school districts the next year anyway. That's the only real thing she ever said in therapy — the only sentence that could in any way be peeled open and analyzed.

Other than her friendship with Kassidy, I recalled that at age ten or eleven, Ava talked about wanting to get married early and have kids. I found it unusual — do ten-year-old boys do that? At the time, I believed she saw marriage and family as a way out of loneliness. I was certainly familiar with that concept. I was an expert on wanting to have my own kids to love and to love me back.

The waiting room door opened. Dr. Stern smiled and asked me to join them. I sat next to Ava on the couch, both of us across from Dr. Stern in his big, comfy therapist's chair.

"First, I want you to know that after meeting with your child, I am completely comfortable being your child's therapist. This is what I do, and I've treated many other teens of similar age with variations of this same story, and I know that we can have a good relationship together." That was exactly what I needed to hear. I needed someone not just to take the wheel but to confidently say he was the right person to do so. We were finally in the right place.

"After the two of us have a few more sessions together, I should be able to give you some more specific feedback," he continued.

Take all the time you need, I thought to myself. *This time, we need to get this right. I can't look for yet another therapist.*

"In the meantime, if anything comes up between appointments that you think I should know, please don't hesitate to let me know. If there are any resources you need, or a therapist for yourself, I can help you with that as well."

"I'm okay for now, thank you," I replied. I wasn't okay, but I thought I didn't have time for that.

The car ride back was fairly quiet. I told Ava that Dr. Stern seemed nice, and I liked him. Ava agreed. I decided then that I was going to give Ava and Dr. Stern a month or two to talk before I asked Dr. Stern what his thoughts were, and that I was not going to push Ava to tell me what they talked about. That morning, I had written in my journal:

> I'm getting not just more used to the new Aydin but developing a fondness for him — almost like having a new baby that you are figuring out.... Today at 5 we meet with the new therapist at the LA Gender Center. I hope this therapist works out. I hope it ends up being someone he can talk to and figure things out with for a while.

I was ready to start seeing my baby in a new light, yet within a week, I found myself frustrated and impatient again. I needed to know whether or not she was definitely transgender. I could not move on until I knew.

My entire life, I've always tried to control everything. Here I was faced with a giant thing that I could not control, that no one could. One day in Sephora, I saw two trans girls with heavy makeup on, laughing together. I couldn't help noticing them. Immediately, I got sad. *I don't want people to look at Aydin and notice him as different right away*, I thought. *I don't want this life for him.* What exactly was "this life" in my mind? A life that was limited by being transgender.

On another day, I walked into Anthropologie and saw a salesman who had a beard, but who was very flamboyant in his style, wearing women's booties and dangly earrings. Again, I thought, *Why can't Aydin just be über gay and weird and fun and his own person like this guy?* And then Ava and I got into an argument over picking her courses for sophomore year, and within a couple days I found myself being her advocate again.

During freshman year, Ava was in men's choir. She loved to sing, but in February, when it came time to choose her elective courses for sophomore year, she said she wanted to quit choir and take an extra math class instead. She didn't want to audition for the advanced coed choir group called the Madrigals. If she tried out and didn't make it, she'd automatically be assigned to another year of men's choir. "You love to sing. Why would you take an extra math class? Math is not a real elective. You have to try out," I told her.

"He doesn't have to try out if he doesn't want to. Let him pick what he wants. It's his decision," Babak countered.

I was pissed that I was the one who was taking care of 95 percent of things, yet Ava and her dad were siding against me. And I was mad because I knew why she didn't want to continue in choir: it was because of the required outfit for boys for concerts, which was a white dress shirt, black dress pants, black tie, belt, and shoes. The girls wore a long black dress with black tights and black Mary Jane shoes. I was trying to get her to admit why she didn't want to try out, and she just kept saying, "I just don't." After a door-slamming fight, I tried again the next day.

"You don't have to try out for Madrigals if you tell me the truth about why you don't want to. I think you don't want to try out because you don't want to wear the boy clothes to the concerts anymore."

"All right. Fine. That's the reason."

"What if I email your choir teacher and counselor privately, and ask if they can make an exception for you? What if I get them to agree that you can wear a white shirt with a long black skirt instead of pants for the concerts? Will you audition then?"

"But still, if I don't make the Madrigals, I'll automatically be put in men's choir. I don't want to be in a group called men's choir anymore," she countered.

"I promise that if you don't make the Madrigals, I won't let them put you in men's choir. I'll make them switch you to an extra math class or another elective."

"Okay. If I don't have to wear the clothes, then I'll try out," she conceded.

The next morning, I found myself advocating for her in school for the first time. In all the other situations, like changing for PE, she had taken care of it herself. I emailed the choir teacher and the counselor:

> As you may have noticed, Aydin has been wearing only gender-neutral or feminine clothing for the last few months. He is having some gender dysphoria, and he is seeing a therapist who is helping him with exploring his gender identity. His discomfort with wearing men's clothing is so great right now that he would rather not audition for the Madrigals although he loves to sing. We don't know what is going to happen. We don't know if he will come to school next year as a girl or stay a boy. We just know that we need to support him through this time.

I asked them if they would make an exception to the dress code for concerts, and her choir teacher emailed me back a couple of options, including just wearing the dress that the girls wore. When I told Ava, she was excited about trying out for Madrigals. She started practicing her audition songs immediately. For the first time in months, I felt good about myself as a mother, felt like I was being proactive and taking care of my child. I wasn't convinced that any of this was permanent, but I knew I was doing the right thing that day.

Within a few days, Ava was back in my bedroom with another question. "Mom, I bought this sports bra, and the straps show on my shoulders. I wanted to see if you think it's okay that I wear it to school." She held up a white sports bra with three crisscrossing rows of bright orange straps across the back. She had already been wearing sports bras hidden under her clothes for some time, but now everyone would be able to tell she was wearing them.

"I don't know. I'll have to ask your dad first." My immediate thought was that she was just trying to push the envelope again and draw more attention to herself at school, rather than assert her femininity. It wasn't until later that I reflected on the bravery of wearing bras with visible straps as a high school freshman who was still considered a boy.

Late one night, I was feeling a little sad and simultaneously grateful for my kids. I always said I could recognize each of my kids with my eyes closed by listening to their breathing as they slept. I decided to peek into each of their rooms and watch them breathe for a few minutes before going to bed. I peeked into Armon's room first, then closed his door. Then I opened Ava's door and saw her lying in bed.

The comforter was pulled halfway up her chest. She was sleeping on her right side, facing the door, with her arms under her head. She was sleeping in a sports bra but no top. I was taken aback. Who sleeps in a bra if they don't have to? And no one could see her. You don't sleep in a sports bra in the privacy of your own room in order to get attention, I realized. You do it to feel like a woman, to be a woman. She stirred and opened her eyes at the light from the hallway streaming into her room. "It's just me, honey, I'm just checking on everyone sleeping. Everything's okay," I said, and she closed her eyes again. I watched her for a few more seconds and then shut her door. I walked to Shayda's room and watched her for a little and then went to bed.

I messaged my sisters the next morning, "I found him sleeping in a sports bra." My younger sister agreed with me that you don't sleep in a sports bra to get attention — you do it to feel like a girl. It was another lightbulb moment for me, another step toward acceptance of what seemed to be happening. Even if this was just a phase Ava was going through, my child was having gender dysphoria — believing she was a girl. I let her wear the bras. A couple of days later, I found myself teaching Ava how to hand-wash her bras in the sink, just as my mother had taught me thirty years before.

Ava hand-washed her bras for a little bit, but then, being your typical lazy teenager, she started putting them in her laundry basket, where Rosa would find them, wash them, and lay them back on her bed. Rosa had started as our babysitter when Shayda was just six months old and I was going back to work. Although we didn't need a babysitter anymore, she had been with us for so long that I never had the heart to let her go. When the kids got older, she worked fewer hours as a general helper and housekeeper.

Rosa saw it all, from nail polish to wearing dresses and everything in between. She never asked any questions or expressed any surprise about what was going on. It must have been obvious what was happening. Maybe she, too, thought, *Well, there has always been something going on with this kid, some sadness or something that no one could quite put a finger on.* So maybe she concluded, *Oh, this is what it has been about all along.*

Many times in the past, I had come home from work and Rosa had said to me, "Aydin is sad today again. He's in his room in bed." I would roll my eyes and say, "Okay, I'll check on him," tired of it, knowing that we wouldn't get to the bottom of it. Later on, when Ava came out to everyone, I told Rosa that we were calling Aydin by the name Ava now, but I don't think she quite understood. She kept calling her by her birth name for a while, and then one day she just asked Ava, "Should I call you Ava now?" And that was it. Within a couple of months, I occasionally heard her calling Ava "*muñeca*" (doll), an endearment she had used for Shayda since she was a baby. We never actually had a conversation in which I told her that Ava was a girl now, because Rosa had witnessed it from the start. She had probably found Ava's makeup in her drawers long before I did.

On February 11, 2018, I attended my second Transforming Family meeting, and I took Ava for her first one. Babak had stayed home with Shayda, not wanting to leave her alone for hours on a Sunday. I anticipated that one of two things would happen: either Ava would go in the teen and older group and decide, "Wait a second, this is not me, I'm not these people, I'm not trans, I'm just confused" — or else she would feel quite the opposite, that she belonged. For the meeting, she redid her nails and put on a light pink H&M knit dress with her olive-green suede boots. Her makeup was a little heavier than what she dared to apply for school.

We walked in together, both of us a little nervous. Looking around, I noticed how many of the kids had colored hair — blue or purple or green. I remembered how many hair colors she had gone through the year before. This must be an early form of self-expression as different or other for a lot of these kids, I thought, a way of experimenting with getting out of the look they've always had.

We were divided into groups of parents, young kids, siblings, and teens and older. The parent group was subdivided into parents of prepuberty and postpuberty kids. I took one last look at Ava's face before we were separated. I couldn't tell whether it expressed nervous excitement or plain old nervousness.

In my parents' subgroup, I asked, "As a parent, you want to protect your child, so how do you know when is the right time after they tell you something like this to start considering hormones? My kid has gone through so many different phases, and he gets unusually preoccupied with different topics, but it's always temporary. He's always had difficulty making friends and seems to be looking for a place to belong. How long do you wait before knowing it's not a phase, six months or a year or what?" I tried to avoid using the terms *son* or *daughter* or *he* or *she* this time.

One of the group moderators was Dr. Karen Neider, a physician from the CHLA Center for Transyouth Health and Development. Her response made me feel I was hindering rather than protecting my child by waiting. "Parents will put their kids on antidepressants, hoping that's the answer. They'll put their kids on stimulants, thinking ADHD is the reason their kid's grades are plummeting. Puberty blockers and hormones have fewer side effects than antidepressants and stimulants. Give your kid what they actually need. While *you* are waiting to get comfortable with this, your kid is suffering."

I thought about what she was saying. As a pediatrician, I had seen many parents wait to bring their children in for an appointment until they were at the breaking point or in a crisis situation with depression or deteriorating school performance due to possible ADHD. Then they would ask that I put a child on medication on the first visit. When I explained that these diagnoses and medications should not be taken lightly, that I would need to refer them to a psychiatrist for further evaluation, I had often been met with frustration that I couldn't solve their problem that day. Why are so many parents not afraid of antidepressants or stimulants, but so afraid of hormones? Why was I so afraid of puberty blockers, the effects of which are completely reversible? Why was I afraid of hormones, the effects of which are mostly reversible?

During this meeting, there was a lot of talk about the higher incidence of autism and Asperger's in trans kids, and about how many of them have very high IQs. I didn't know Ava's exact IQ, but her unusual intelligence was obvious to everyone. She had never had an official autism spectrum diagnosis, but she had always seemed socially out of place — although in the past year, she had been making more friends.

Another mother came up to me as we were leaving the room after the meeting. "You know, your story reminded me of my child's. My child had a hard time making friends and is very smart and always seemed a little socially awkward, and then once we accepted her being trans and she came out, all the social oddities and awkwardness went away. Your story just reminded me of my kid. I just wanted you to know. I don't know your child, but it's not as scary as you think. You're here. You guys will figure this out." She was very sweet. While Dr. Neider's comment had made me feel guilty, what this mother said stuck with me. After that second meeting I finally decided to ask Ava's pediatrician (my colleague Vicki) to refer her to the CHLA Center for Transyouth Health and Development as a patient.

As I left the room, I spotted Ava outside. Before we even made eye contact, I saw a look on her face that said, "These are my people." There was an excitement, an awakening, a realization. She hadn't gone and said, "Oh, this isn't me." She had identified, she had felt like she belonged. When she walked over to me, she couldn't get her questions out fast enough, "When is the next meeting? I want to go to all their meetings. Can we please go to all their meetings?"

"We'll go anytime we can, as long as we don't have a family conflict."

"But it's just once a month. You just have to make it a priority," she pleaded.

"You have two other siblings. I promise to bring you every time I can, but I can't promise we will make every one. We will do our best."

On the car ride home, she told me about the meeting for teens to young adults. After about fifteen minutes, they had broken up into MTF (male to female), FTM (female to male), and nonbinary groups. Her group hadn't actually spent much time talking about trans issues or experiences: they had discussed movies and media, friends and schools. She had enjoyed simply being with a group of girls like herself and being treated and seen as a girl. She was happy, she was hopeful. I was happy for her, worried for all of us.

Within a few Transforming Family sessions, I changed. As I came to my own acceptance and understanding of what was going on with Ava, I went from being the one crying and seeking advice to the one listening and offering advice to other new parents. I heard so many stories like mine: "We had no idea.…We didn't know.…There were never any signs.…This came out of the blue." And the more I heard those stories, the less I feared that Ava might just be going through a phase, and the less alone I felt, the more confident I felt about her starting the process of medical transition. Those meetings, which I so resisted for a while, ultimately changed everything for us. At a certain point, I realized there was nothing more Ava could have done to convince me.

I had to hear other mothers tell their stories.

Within a few days of Ava's first Transforming Family meeting, Babak and I had another talk with her. Strange as it seemed, she still had not told her siblings anything. She was still their brother Aydin, cross-dressing and experimenting with makeup for fun or self-expression. We told her that we needed to start thinking about telling her siblings. "I know," Ava said. "Also, Dr. Stern and a few of my friends who know have been calling me Lucy for a while, so maybe at the same time as we tell them, you guys can start calling me Lucy, too."

The name Aydin, which is originally a Turkish boys' name, is used as a girls' name among Iranians: Babak's cousin's wife is named Aydin. We tried to get Ava to consider keeping her name the same, since it was gender-neutral — in our eyes, anyway. "No," she said. "I still associate that name with my old self. Eventually, I don't want to have any association with my old self."

Babak and I had been talking about the name Lucy on our own, as we both suspected after the Starbucks cup episode that she was using it. Neither one of us could imagine calling her Lucy. For me, it was because Lucy does not sound in any way Middle Eastern, and having her change her name to something that did not fit with the rest of our family names seemed like she would not just be changing her gender expression but leaving our family. I could not imagine introducing someone to my kids and saying, "These are my kids, Armon, Shayda, and Lucy." I felt like it would draw even more attention to the fact that there was something different about her.

With Babak beside me, I told Ava, "We don't want you to get too attached to the name Lucy. We can come up with a list of names that are both Farsi and American, and we can see if there is a name that all three of us can agree on. You are still our child. We are still a family." Ava got upset. Later, in our bedroom, Babak, who had seemed to be handling things better than I had, broke down over considering a name change. He cried, his body shaking. He couldn't imagine not calling her Aydin, or his nickname for her, which was simply Ay (pronounced "eye"). He couldn't imagine not calling out "Ar, Ay, Shay, come downstairs." He asked me if I remembered the movie *Eternal Sunshine of the Spotless Mind* and told me he was afraid that just as in that movie, the memories of our little boy would slip away and become confused, and we wouldn't even know which ones were real and which were not.

I realized that during this whole process, Babak and I had been alternating the role of being the strong parent. When one of us was breaking down, the other was strong and optimistic. Then some event would reverse our roles. For most of this journey, Babak had been the strong and optimistic parent, but now it was my turn. I also thought back to all the ups and downs of our relationship of more than twenty years, and all the times that I had wanted to be out of it. For most of our years together, Babak had had issues with mood swings, being quick to anger and susceptible to mild depression. I had often felt that the kids and I needed to tiptoe around his moods, and that I needed to make up for his unpredictability by being the steadily happy and optimistic parent. Babak seemed to take my stability for granted, allowing himself to wallow in his own moods while knowing I would be there for the kids. He knew I would never leave the marriage as long as we had kids at home. There had been many times in my marriage when I had felt that the one thing I couldn't control was Babak's moods, that maybe it would have been easier if I had been on my own with the kids and I could control everything.

After I started running, I changed profoundly, and Babak saw it, felt it. For the first time, he realized the confidence, sense of identity, and calm that I gained from running might also lead me to leave our marriage. When he saw me change, he decided to change himself, too — not just because he was afraid that I would leave, but also because he had become tired of himself. Over the last couple of years, he had undergone his own transformation. He had started meditating, reading, training for triathlons. By the time of our yoga retreat in Thailand together, he was a new person, and our marriage was the strongest it had ever been.

Despite this turning point, I sometimes thought back to all the low points of our years together. Now with Ava's transition, I thought that it had been worth sticking through all those challenges, because this was one thing I wasn't sure I could have handled on my own, without someone who felt the same profound sense of loss that I did. I knew that this should not be a sense of loss. I knew that I had not lost a child. I knew that was not the politically correct way to put it. But that was what it felt like.

On February 19, 2018, we finally decided to tell Armon and Shayda that Ava was transgender. I didn't want Armon and Shayda to later feel that they were the last ones to find out, and as I was starting to believe this to be real, I didn't want there to be a secret — a lie — in our family. We still had not agreed on a name, so we were still calling her Aydin and using male pronouns. We called Armon and Shayda down to the family room. Ava sat next to me, while Babak sat in another chair. Armon and Shayda were on opposite ends of the couch across the room, looking at each other as if wondering which one had done something to precipitate a family meeting. Ava wanted me to tell them. "We're going to talk about something that for now is going to remain private and in our family. You've probably noticed the changes in Aydin over the last year, but these changes aren't just because Aydin likes to wear girly clothes. Aydin is a girl on the inside. He is transgender. We wanted to tell you because eventually, this is something we'll share with everyone, and we want you to know first and have time to get used to it before everyone knows."

Armon didn't show much of a reaction at all. "Okay," he said. "Is that it?" He seemed relieved that the meeting was about something he had already figured out on his own, and he wanted to leave. Shayda, on the other hand, was completely surprised. I guess she had thought that Ava was wearing dresses and skirts for fun. At eleven years old, Shayda was in the peak of her unicorn phase. On Shayda's last birthday, all of her presents were unicorn-themed: unicorn onesie pajamas, a unicorn pillow, a unicorn purse, and a mug from her aunt Laila that said, "Be a unicorn in a field of horses." She thought of her older brother Aydin as a unicorn. Sometimes she took pictures of "my brother Aydin" wearing makeup or a skirt and texted them to her friends with a string of unicorn emojis. Shayda already knew Ava was bisexual — Ava had told her that months before — but she had no idea about her being trans.

As we explained the situation, Shayda initially gasped and got excited. "You mean I'm going to have a sister?" Then, a couple of minutes later, she started crying as she realized that it meant that she was losing her brother. You could see a wave of emotions and realizations going through her. She came up to Ava while crying and hugged her and said, "I love you." Ava didn't give much of a response, barely hugging Shayda in return. She seemed to be waiting for more of a response from Armon, the one she had always idolized, but she didn't get one.

"We're trying to agree on a new girl name that we can all call Aydin, and hopefully we'll decide on that soon," I continued, doing all the talking for Babak and myself. "Once we have done that, you'll see Baba and me calling him by the new name at least at home, and using *she* and *her* at home. When we start doing that, you guys can do it, too, or you can take some time to get used to it first. At some point, Aydin will go by the new name and female pronouns to everyone, and once he is out to everyone, you'll have to start using the new name and pronouns if you haven't done it yet. We wanted to tell you now so that you would have some time to get used to this before Aydin comes out to everyone."

"You and Baba are picking the new name, right? You guys should be picking it," Armon finally voiced an opinion.

"We're still working on the new name together, with Aydin," I answered.

"You guys should definitely still be picking the name. You guys are still the parents," Armon reiterated. This made Ava even more upset, feeling that Armon was not supporting her at all. But Armon's lack of emotional response was a good thing, although Ava could not see it at the time. He had already figured things out on his own, and it really didn't make any difference to him. Their relationship had not changed at all since Armon started piecing things together.

We finished the family meeting by emphasizing the importance of not telling other people until Ava came out to the world, our concern mostly being about Shayda and not Armon. They handled it all pretty well. Shayda experienced a little jealousy and discomfort going from being my only girl to being one of two. I think she asked me once if she was still my favorite daughter, as I had often jokingly called her because I thought she was the only one I had. I told her that I understood her feelings about all the big changes, but that I did not have a favorite daughter anymore, or favorite girl in the world. Sometimes, I felt that Ava resented Shayda over certain things, such as having breasts or being seen as my only daughter for twelve years, but overall, the sibling rivalry was not more than there would be in any other family. While my sisters and I rarely had any sibling rivalry among us, through my years of medical practice, I'd taken care of hundreds of families, and I'd seen the degree to which changes in the family could affect the dynamics between siblings. Considering all the changes we had been through, the stability in my kids' relationships was pretty remarkable.

At the end of February, I had another big turning point. I stumbled on a video posted on a friend's Facebook wall. This was a casual friend who did not know about our family situation. It was a twelve-minute video from the Moth storytelling website, a story narrated by a woman named Cybele Abbett.*

I watched Cybele tell the story of her son, born assigned female based on genitalia, who around the start of high school told his mom that he was gay. Then, a couple of weeks later, he told her, "Actually, Mom, I'm not gay, I'm a boy." As I watched the video, I imagined my future self for the first time. I saw myself not only accepting all of this but being proud of making this journey with my child. I felt chills. It was one of the first times that I thought, *Maybe one day I can embrace all of this and truly see him as a girl.* This liberal, beautiful, caring, involved mother was telling my story and Ava's — with the genders reversed, but fundamentally the same. As I saw her go through the reactions of shock, grief, acceptance, and pride, I could picture myself standing there and saying the same thing one day.

I watched that video over and over. I sent it to my sisters and to my parents. I sent it to Jake and Carmelo and all my good friends who knew what was going on, and I said, "This is me...she is me...this is how I feel...this is what is happening to me." This mother's progression of emotions was my progression too, and I could see a light at the end of the tunnel, a day when I would be not just at peace but proud and an advocate.

I became a little obsessed with Cybele. I managed to find her by looking through all the comments on the video. She had sent supportive replies to some of the trans people commenting and ignored all the hateful comments. I messaged her through Facebook:

---

*   Cybele Abbett, "Leaping Forward," video available at www.facebook.com/hey irisdotcom/videos/1396614843739198, accessed January 21, 2020. An audio version is available on the Moth website: https://themoth.org/storytellers/cybele-abbett, accessed January 7, 2020.

Dear Cybele: I hope that it's okay that I contact you this way. I just watched your Moth video and it was like a gift made specifically for me....I have a 14-year-old who a year ago told us he is bisexual and then 8 months ago said he is a trans girl....Your video was the first time that I really heard a story of a parent finding out when their child is a teen that I 100% connected with. Everything in the media is about kids who present as toddlers or a little older. I felt like every word you said could come out of my mouth....I have gone to some support group meetings, but no one else's story has resonated with me as much as listening to yours.

Cybele responded, saying she'd be happy to talk to me. We arranged a time to talk, and this beautiful stranger spent forty-five minutes on the phone with me. She told me that one thing that she did not mention in the video was that at every difficult decision point, she would ask herself, "'Am I making this decision based on love or based on fear?' I decided to make decisions based on love." And I thought that was just such valuable advice. Because every time I was holding back on taking any next step with Ava, it was out of fear and not of love. The loving choice would be to look at my child and see what they needed now and go with that. The fearful choice would be to look at my child and say, "But if I let them do this, what if this other thing happens down the line?" After that I resolved to try my best to make decisions based on love and not fear.

When we were talking on the phone, despite hearing me refer to Ava as my son and using male pronouns, Cybele was bold enough to say, in a kind, gentle voice, "I'm just going to refer to her as your daughter in our conversation." She used *she/her* pronouns. And she did it in a way that wasn't upsetting to me, because there was clearly such a good intention behind her words and her actions. Spending forty-five minutes talking to me, years after this video was made, was an incredibly generous thing to do — although now I know that I would take the time to talk to any parent going through the same thing.

After that conversation with Cybele, I thought a lot about acting out of fear versus love. I asked myself, *What if there were no fear or hate in the world? How would I parent differently then? Why am I letting the fear and hate in the world create so much noise in my head that I'm not listening to my child? What if I turned the volume from that fear and hate noise down, from a ten to a three? What would I do then? With a newborn, you take care of them instinctively, minute to minute, and address their immediate needs. What if I stop projecting into the future and take care of my child's immediate needs based on love?*

Listening to Cybele, and parents at Transforming Family, is what changed things for me. I had to hear the parent's perspective from others who had gone through the same thing; that's the reason for any of us to share our story. And every person I sent her video to also understood when they watched it. They were moved.

On March 1, 2018, Babak finally had phone conversations with his siblings and parents in which he told them everything. They all already knew a fair amount of what was going on, but now Babak told them that he was sure Ava was trans, that this was not a phase, and that we would be supporting her through her transition. His siblings were very supportive. He did not ask his parents for a response. Babak told them he wanted to just let them know and give them some time to digest the news, and that they would talk about it more later.

By March, I also decided that it was time for me to sit down with Dr. Stern. I had given him and Ava enough time and sessions for him to be able to give me at least some preliminary thoughts, and I wanted to hear what he had to say so I could start to move on. I wrote in my journal before we met:

> I want to ask him his thoughts on Aydin so far — if he thinks based on what he knows so far and his experience, if Aydin is trans. We'll have to see what he says. I think he is going to say yes, he is. And if he does, I want to know what I should do

next and at what rate he wants to progress.... I'm ready to hear what he has to say — ready to hear what someone who has just been working with my child for a couple of months, as opposed to me who has known him his whole life, ready to hear what he has to say and accept it and move on. It's hard as a mother to in a way give over your child to someone and have them tell you about your child, but it's time to accept that and get over these expectations of what as a mother I should know. Here we go...time for the next step.

Giving up control was a recurring theme for me that year. It was something I had long needed to learn to do, but giving up control of my child was not easy.

That day, Dr. Stern met with Ava for about half an hour, and then Ava came out and took a seat in the waiting room. I walked into Dr. Stern's office and sat on the big brown leather couch. He sat across from me in his chair, legs crossed, leaning forward, hands clasped together, ready to deliver his verdict. "I believe that you have a girl." He paused for a few seconds to let me absorb the impact of that statement and went on, "I don't say that because of what she wears or if she is putting on makeup. I say that because when she walks in this room and we close that door and she gets to be seen as a girl and accepted as a girl for fifty minutes, her entire demeanor changes, her face lights up. She is so happy to be in a space once a week where she can be who she is."

He reinforced his view by stating that, on the basis of his experience, he thought the chance of this being a phase was very low. He reiterated that taking care of trans teens and young adults was what he did, and he was confident in his assessment. He was very gentle but sure and certain in the way he delivered it. Just as I had felt on my first meeting with Dr. Stern, I felt this was what I needed to hear. I needed an expert to give me an opinion and take the burden of making decisions and determinations off my shoulders.

Dr. Stern asked, "What do you think of what I told you, and how do you feel?"

"I was expecting that you would say this. I actually told my sisters that we were meeting today and that I was expecting you to tell me Aydin is a girl." Then some tears started to trickle down my face. "Obviously, this is hard. Obviously, no parent wants this for their child. But I will be okay, and I just need to know so that we can move forward and I know what to do for him next. I'll be okay. We'll all be okay."

"I think you should consider a therapist for yourself. It is normal and expected for you to go through your own grieving and acceptance process, and it will help to have someone to talk to. I can provide you with some names of therapists for you."

"I don't think I need that. I have my husband and family and friends. I'm surrounded by people who are accepting of all of this. I just needed to know. The hardest part has been not knowing. But I trust your assessment, and so now that I know, I think I can move forward."

He reached over to the bookshelf behind him and handed me the book *The Transgender Child: A Handbook for Families and Professionals* by Stephanie Brill and Rachel Pepper, offering to lend me his copy. I said I would order my own copy, and he could save his for another parent who might need to borrow it. Cybele had sent me a link to the same book and told me it helped her immensely. I wiped my eyes, composed myself, and joined Ava in the waiting room.

I wish I could recall the car ride home with Ava that day. I think I must have told her about our conversation, and she must have reached over and hugged me in the car or held my hand. Often after therapy in the car ride home, she would lean over from the passenger seat and hug me while I was driving and lean her head on my shoulder. She'd hold my hand. It was her way of saying, "I know this is difficult for you, but I love you and I appreciate all that is being done for me, and I'm happy."

She would mother me in the car rides home rather than the other way around.

I ordered the book. When I started reading it, there were many points where I felt guilty. I underlined several passages stressing that when your child asks you to refer to them as the other gender or use other pronouns at home, you should, that you should allow them to express themselves and not oppose it — that you should believe them when they come to you. I felt so bad about what we had done, about the period when we hadn't believed Ava or had refused to call her by a girl name or female pronouns.

The book talked about the three times in life when trans people typically first present. The first phase is early childhood, from toddler to pre-puberty, but about 50 percent of transgender people do not present until around puberty or later. Fifty percent! The second phase is preteen and early adolescence:

> The next typical time for transgender identity to emerge is just before and during puberty, so depending on the child, between 9 and 14 years old. At this age, children begin to experience hormonal and physical changes toward maturation, and huge alerts go off in their brains.... [P]arents may notice something amiss with their child and take them to a therapist for withdrawal, acting out, depression, or self-mutilation.

The third phase is late adolescence:

> The third typical time for transgender self-realization during childhood is the end of adolescence, when the other parts of the self have emerged more fully and gender identity becomes clear. Before that point, many teenagers try on different sexualities to see what fits best, not realizing that the inner mismatch is not about sexual orientation but rather about gender.*

---

*   Stephanie Brill and Rachel Pepper, *The Transgender Child: A Handbook for Families and Professionals* (San Francisco, CA: Cleis Press, 2008), 18, 20.

When I read those two passages, my heart stopped, and I cried. I took pictures of them and sent them to my sisters. This was my kid. Ava started puberty early, so she presented in midadolescence. She started out by trying on different sexualities and saying she was bisexual before realizing the issue was gender. Reading this I kept thinking, *Why doesn't anyone ever tell you this stuff?* The general population aside, why did I not learn anything about this during pediatric residency? I kept remembering our family room conversation, when I insisted that Ava couldn't be trans because she hadn't had signs in childhood. I had been dead wrong. My lack of knowledge had made me not listen, not believe my child.

I thought back to Ms. Garcia, the school psychologist for the elementary and middle schools in our district. Over the years, Ms. Garcia had become well acquainted with our family. Ava had met with her regularly in second grade, after saying she wished she could go to bed and not wake up. Over the next five years, she met with Ava periodically when some classroom or playground incident landed Ava back in her office. I wondered if in any of their sessions, Ava might have said anything that someone better trained in recognizing gender dysphoria in children would have picked up on. If I found Ms. Garcia or Ava's first-grade teacher, Ms. Katz, and told them she was now saying that she was transgender, would they be surprised, or would they think, *Oh, that all makes sense now?*

The truth is that nobody working with kids is properly trained on gender issues, be it teachers, psychologists, or pediatricians. I can't blame Ms. Garcia or Ava's teachers or other therapists for not picking up on clues any more than I can blame myself.

After that meeting with Dr. Stern, I decided that I would start practicing calling Ava my daughter and using female pronouns in my diary, even though we still hadn't settled on a name. I wrote:

> Today I'll start by practicing referring to Aydin as she...as my daughter. I'll start by practicing it in private in writing. Today, I start again. I will try to decrease my worry and

think positively and I will put a certain amount of trust in the universe...that the universe will take care of my baby who is kind and sweet and has a big heart. I will trust that the universe will give back love and kindness to her big heart. I will breathe and I will be and I'll trust and accept and move forward with what is to come.

The next day, we were still having difficulty on settling on a name. She still wanted the name Lucy. She said that one night a year before, it had just sort of come to her, and Babak and I wondered whether we should just go with it. But to me, it just didn't feel like my child's name. It did not fit in with our family. I didn't want her to stand out from my other kids. Two days later we were in the family room, with the three kids sitting on the couch, and at a glance, Ava was starting to look more like Shayda.

A few days later we participated in the Pasadena Triathlon. Babak and I had done it the year before. It was a reverse triathlon, with the run first, then the bike segment, then the swim. Ava had expressed an interest in doing a triathlon with us months before, and since this one was a simple one with a pool swim rather than an open-water swim, we said she could do it. We had registered her without thinking about what she would wear for the swim. Ava decided that just for this triathlon, she would just wear men's swim trunks. I told her that she could wear a rash-guard top if she wanted to, but for whatever reason, she said no. At this point, Ava was looking more like a girl, or at least like a gender-nonconforming person, in everyday clothes, but that day at the starting line for the run, in her men's swim trunks and shirt, she just looked like a boy growing out his hair. I realized that I was getting so used to her new look that she didn't look like herself to me when she dressed like a boy.

A couple weeks later, we received a link to the website hosting the official photos from the event. Looking at a picture of Ava when she had just gotten out of the pool and was crossing the finish line in trunks and no top, I was surprised by the characteristically male body I saw — a thin male body with washboard abs and broad shoulders, not a body that anyone would see for a second as "a girl" or "gender-nonconforming." The picture didn't look like my baby anymore. It looked like someone else. It showed what she was hiding underneath her clothes and how much she was changing her appearance by putting on sports bras and women's clothing. I thought about how she saw her own body in the shower or whenever she changed clothes. I worried, *How in the hell is this body going to eventually get feminized?* I thought about how I was starting to actually see my new child, or I guess the new version of my child — my daughter.

CHAPTER 8

METAMORPHOSIS

Babak and I sat in bed late at night, looking at each other. For the past nine months, our bedroom had stopped being a sanctuary and become a place where decisions were made after whispered discussions. "Now that we have the reassurance from Dr. Stern's official assessment, I don't think we have any reason to hold back Aydin from physical transition any longer," I told Babak.

"I didn't even need his official assessment to know that," he replied. I had already made Ava's first appointment at the Children's Hospital transgender center in anticipation, but they had a months-long waiting list, and that visit was still two months away. But we could proceed with some of the nonmedical aspects of transition.

Because of our Middle Eastern background, our kids have all been early bloomers, so at the age of fourteen, Ava already had complete, thick facial hair. She was shaving aggressively every morning in an attempt to look more feminine, leaving her face red and raw, but by noon, her five-o'clock shadow was already visible. It was time to try laser hair removal. I called a few places, but they all had a minimum age limit of sixteen. I emailed a dermatologist colleague and explained the situation. The dermatologist said that they would be happy to do the procedure, but because

Ava's puberty was not complete, it would probably take double the usual number of sessions. She gave us an appointment for the next day.

Ava had early dismissal from school, and I was off from work. I picked her up and took her to Eataly in Century City Mall so we could have a nice lunch together before her appointment. I also wanted to discuss settling on a name yet again. Weeks before, we had given her a list of names that are both Farsi and English — Ava, Farah, Sara — but she was still set on Lucy. It was a perfect Los Angeles afternoon, and the hostess sat us at an outside table on the balcony. The waiter initially saw Ava from behind, with her hair almost shoulder-length and her bra strap showing. He walked up and asked, "Can I get you ladies anything to drink?" Then Ava looked up at him, and the waiter's face turned red. "Oh, I'm sorry, I just saw you from behind and…" He trailed off. He didn't know what to say. He didn't know if she was a boy or a girl.

I quickly smiled at the waiter and said, "That's okay. I'll take a glass of the rosé, and she will just have a water."

This was how it was going to be for a while. During this in-between phase, people couldn't tell if she was a trans girl or a boy in feminine clothing, growing out his hair. I told Ava there would be a lot of people making mistakes in addressing her, but if they were well-intentioned, like the waiter, then we'd just have to get used to smiling and moving on. "I know, Mom, this happens to me all the time. It's fine."

Just a few days before, we had been at an Aldo shoe store together, looking at the women's shoes. A saleswoman had walked up and said, "Can I get you ladies any shoes?" with full confidence, despite seeing Ava's face. It had made Ava very happy. In all these little interactions, I held my breath, waiting to see how she was going to be addressed and if she was going to get upset. I had to learn to let that go very quickly. Overall, she seemed to be handling it better than I was. Or maybe she had just learned to hide her feelings because she had to deal with being misgendered every day.

She'd been misgendered one way or another her whole life.

Over lunch, I brought up the topic of names and why it was important to me that her name not stand out from the names of the rest of our family. I told her that my own father had wanted to name my younger sister Ava, but my mom had preferred all three of her daughters to have names that started with P. In fact our names didn't just start with P: they started with *Par*, as does my mother's name Parvin. Par means "feather"; Paria means "fairy" or "angel," and Parimah means "beautiful fairy." Parastou is Farsi for the swallow bird, and Parvin refers to a group of stars. Names having a meaning or a rhyme or a certain rhythm is customary in Persian culture, and although we had not stuck to a pattern in naming our children, each name we chose had significance. Armon means "your ideals or aspirations." Shayda means "passion," but to me, her name refers to someone who does everything with passion. Aydin means "clarity." Ava means "a fulfilling sound or voice" — so it seemed appropriate for Ava, who has a beautiful, deep singing voice.

Maybe because we were going to her first laser appointment that day, a definitive marker on moving forward, she agreed to the name Ava. I reiterated that we were okay with Lucy as a middle name in addition to Ava: her friends could call her Lucy if she wanted, and her family would call her Ava, or everyone could call her Ava and she could have Lucy as a middle name, to honor the name she first identified with. "No, Mom. Just Ava. Armon and Shayda don't have middle names, you and Baba don't, so Ava it is." She smiled.

So on March 8, 2018, over burrata pizza and cacio e pepe at Eataly, she became Ava. We drank a toast to her new name. From that moment, I started using the name Ava and *she/her* pronouns to go with it. One day later, I wrote in my journal that I missed her old name already — I missed writing it and saying it. She would remain Aydin in school and with people who didn't know for a while longer, and so when I had a chance to still say her old name in those contexts, I enjoyed hearing it come out of my mouth — pausing to relish the sound of it — and also felt conflicted. I fantasized about going to the shower and turning the water on full blast and screaming it, but I didn't do it. When I had to write her legal name on a form, I'd slow down my pen and watch my hand form the name Aydin letter by letter.

When I called my mom to tell her that we had settled on the name Ava, she called out to my dad and said, "You finally got the name Ava. You didn't get it for your daughters, but now you have it for your grand-daughter." That made me happy. The situation wasn't easy for them, but they were doing what they could to show their support. I messaged my sisters to tell them our mom's reaction. They were impressed with how progressive she had become. She had voted for Barack Obama, then Bernie Sanders in the 2016 Democratic primary, then Hillary Clinton, and now this.

Ava's first laser session was one of the worst experiences I've been through. We met with the dermatologist and the nurse, Nancy, who would be the one administering the treatments. They were both very sweet, making Ava feel comfortable and accepted, but the treatment itself was painful. She squeezed my hand, and we both cried. Ava had to take many breaks. I kept asking her if she wanted to just stop, and she kept saying no. I questioned whether I had made a huge mistake in scheduling the appointment. At the same time, seeing her willing to endure that much pain confirmed that her gender identification was real. Ava had always been a chicken with low pain tolerance. She would not have been putting herself through excruciating pain if she wasn't trans — if she was just confused or trying to get attention. Despite all the strides I'd made in believing her, I still needed these reassurances.

I was furious that day, mad at the world. No mother should have to watch their child go through so much pain. I was mad at Babak because I had to be the one to take all this on, sitting through appointments with Ava while he was at work. I was angry about having to make decisions for my child based on a guess of what was best for my child rather than knowing something was necessary. It was one of my hardest moments as a mother, taking my child for an elective procedure and watching her crying in pain. I felt bad for Nancy, who was very patient and had to watch us both cry and keep taking breaks. I wondered if she questioned her role in Ava's laser treatments.

Because of the cost of the treatments, we decided that the dermatology office would do Ava's face, but Babak would do her arms. He did not want to be responsible for doing her face in case she had a bad reaction or hyperpigmentation. For the first session on her arms, Babak used a low setting on the machine, and it apparently went okay. For the second session, he used a higher setting. I went with them. As with the treatment of Ava's face, it led to pain and crying. After that, Babak said he was done. "Take her to whoever and pay whatever is needed, but I'm not doing this to my child."

After five laser face sessions, progress was not good. It worked on her cheeks, but it wasn't doing anything for the chin or goatee area. We were advised to try electrolysis. Ava was nervous because she had heard that electrolysis is more painful. In addition, she would not be able to shave for at least two days before the treatment, and that would be uncomfortable for her while going to school.

The people at the electrolysis center, who have a big trans clientele, were very nice. They explained the entire process and the reasons for not shaving. "For electrolysis, the hair has to actually be long enough that we can grab it and pull it out with the tweezers after the current has passed through the hair follicle base. If we can't see the hair, we can't pull it out," the owner said. "I have teenagers, I understand that your daughter doesn't want to skip shaving on a school day. You either need to schedule around school holidays or wait to do it over the summer." We scheduled a first appointment for a time when she had no school for a couple of days due to a Jewish holiday.

The first electrolysis session was much less painful than the laser treatment. No tears were shed by anyone. Although it became apparent that it would be a very slow process requiring many appointments and costing thousands of dollars, it seemed worth it. I'd pay anything not to have to sit through any more crying sessions.

Through all of this, I knew how fortunate we were to be able to pay for these expensive treatments for Ava, and I never took that good fortune for granted. Transitioning is a huge financial burden for many families, adding extra stress to an already stressful and difficult situation. Some health insurance companies do cover a certain amount of hair removal as part of a gender transition, but getting authorization for these services often requires jumping through many hoops. Hopefully it will become easier over time.

A few days after that first laser session, we were back at another Transforming Family meeting. Once again, I heard new parents in disbelief telling new stories of children not presenting until puberty or later. One of the facilitators commented, "If you are waiting for 100 percent certainty that your child is trans and will stay trans, the 100 percent certainty may never come, just as there is never 100 percent certainty with anything in life. You make the best decisions you can based on what is presenting in front of you now." I thought about certainty and asked Babak about it. "I'm 100 percent sure Ava is trans," he said. "I've been 100 percent sure for at least a few months now. You are the one who hasn't been sure."

I told him that I was 90 percent sure. Now, as I write this, am I at 100 percent yet? I think I'm at 99.9 percent. I'm not sure whether a question mark will always remain. I don't think it will. I imagine it will go away with time.

A few days later, Babak and I found Ava lying on the family room couch, looking sad. We asked her what was wrong. "I'm just worried about my future. I know that I'm not going to get as good a job because I'm trans."

That was the day we realized we needed to change the conversation and narrative in our house. We needed to stop telling Ava that we were worried about her future.

We told her that it wasn't true — that we were optimistic she could get the best job out there. That we would not tolerate negativity about the future from any of our children. We cited some recent examples of trans people in the news. Danica Roem had just become the first openly transgender person elected to the House of Delegates in Virginia. "With your combination of brilliance and having family support with financial backing, there is no limit to what you can do. You can be a trailblazer and pave the way for other people. There is no reason not to be one."

We decided to say goodbye to any negativity immediately. We needed to stop putting negative energy in our home, in our conversations and worried faces, so Ava didn't pick it up. We stopped asking, "Are you sure this is the right thing for you, because you are going to have a hard life ahead?" On the inside, I had the same worries, but as I stopped verbalizing them, I slowly became more optimistic about the possibilities for her future. As Ava started making more friends and I saw her being happier, my worries decreased.

These days, I still worry, but not as much. I worry about Ava's safety, but not so much about the possibility of her being alone or living an unfulfilled life. I know that the trans community is beautiful and accepting and strong, and the parents I meet in Transforming Family are determined that their children will have good futures and be accepted in this world. One of the greatest gifts from this process has been connecting with this wonderful community of families that I would not have otherwise met. As the trans community continues to grow, it will get stronger and stronger.

For spring break, I had planned a trip to New York City to visit my sister Parimah's family. Babak's sister Laila also lives there, so it would be an opportunity to see her as well, although Babak had to stay behind in LA to work. Ava and I had a talk. She didn't know that her aunts knew everything. "What name do you want to go by in New York? If you want, I can tell your aunts that you are a girl and they can call you Ava. They know some of what has been happening anyway, because of your pictures. I know they'll be supportive." She wanted to be Ava.

I called Parimah. "I'm completely okay with telling my kids and everyone calling her that," she said, "but you know, Soha [her four-year-old daughter] is all about what boys do and wear and what girls do and wear these days. She may ask questions or say something that upsets Ava."

I told her not to worry and that Ava realized Soha was only four years old. "We could always tell her that Aydin has a new name, which is Ava, and that she has always been a girl, and she used to dress the way most boys dress, but she is not doing that anymore. That is basically the truth in a nutshell, anyway." We decided to play it by ear.

When we visited, Parimah's three kids were four, two, and just turning one. The one-year-old, Roya, wasn't talking at all, and Ava was excited that Roya would never know her as anyone but Ava. She wanted to teach Roya to say "Ava" as her first word, but that didn't happen. Soha and her two-year-old brother were perfectly fine. Once in a while they'd slip and call her Aydin and then correct themselves. Soha once asked Ava, "If you're a girl, how come you don't wear a bow in your hair?" Ava answered that her hair wasn't long enough (although, given that we put bows on bald babies' heads, Ava had more than enough hair for a bow), but Soha didn't question that and didn't ask anything else. Sometimes, I'd find her looking at Ava as if she had a question in her head, but she never asked any others.

On that trip, Ava was happy. We were all happy. It was exactly what we needed. It was cold in New York, so Ava always had a scarf wrapped around her neck. She loved how the scarf covered her Adam's apple, a part of her body she was very self-conscious about. She would look at herself in store mirrors and say things like "Mom, I look pretty cute. I mean, I'd date myself." I agreed with her. In the American Eagle store, she decided to try some clothes on. She gave the name Ava, which was written on the fitting-room door. I took a picture of it; the first time Ava was written in public.

I had bought tickets for the musical *Dear Evan Hansen* months in advance. It was excellent, second only to *Hamilton* of the shows I've seen. Every teen should see *Dear Evan Hansen* if they can. It's about high school, anxiety, depression, social media, and how getting caught up in a lie can so quickly get out of hand. Ava sat beside me and kept leaning her

Ava's name written in public for the first time, on the American Eagle dressing room door.

head on my shoulder or squeezing my hand. All of us cried. I ugly-cried, overwhelmed by emotion from both the show and from this trip with my children, away from LA.

One day, Ava got sick with some sort of twenty-four-hour bug. She lay around all day with a bad stomachache. Shayda asked if Ava was getting her period, making me realize that she didn't fully understand this thing that she was accepting and going along with. I had to explain it to her better.

While Ava was sick, Armon and I went on a tour of Columbia University alone, just the two of us. It made me realize that I missed alone time with my other kids. I'd spent so much alone time with Ava in car rides to therapy, laser treatments, and lunches together. I had to find some way to have more alone time in LA with Shayda and Armon as well. This transition had taken over our lives. I felt guilty about neglecting Armon and Shayda, guilty about how long it took me to accept Ava, guilty about everything. But the family time in New York City made up for a little of it. And it gave me hope for the day that Ava would be Ava full time in LA as well. One day, everything would feel more settled and back to normal.

One day, we'd no longer be a family in transition, but just a family again.

When we got back to LA, Ava told me that her favorite part of our trip was feeling comfortable walking around the streets of the city. I thought about myself at that age. Growing up in Pittsburgh, I saw New York City as a magical place. My mom's best friend lived in Paramus, New Jersey, but owned a candy store in the city right across from the Macy's on Fifth Avenue. When we visited them, at least once a year, I was free to walk the streets on my own as long as I periodically checked in at the candy store. In the Big Apple, my brown skin did not matter; I blended in with the diverse crowd. I didn't have to try to disappear the way I wanted to in the halls of my high school. I was just one person in the massive crowds, yet at the same time, I was present and visible. I belonged.

These trips, and visits to other big cities like LA and Washington, DC, gave me hope that I wouldn't have to spend my entire life like an outsider but could blend into the melting pot of people and just be myself. Back home in Pittsburgh, I imagined my adult, self-confident self living in a diverse city. Those fantasy visions got me through high school. If I didn't go to parties or to my prom, it didn't matter. My real life was waiting for me in the future.

Now Ava was feeling the same in New York. With her scarf covering her neck and the sheer number of people walking the streets, no one was doing any double takes on seeing her. She blended in. She could be herself. The week in New York gave her the same feeling I had every time I visited New York: *One day in the future, I will blend in.*

On the last day of March, I reflected in my diary about March being the month we settled on Ava's name:

> March, in like a lion, out like a lamb. March has always been my favorite month — the coming of spring, the gradual return to warmth or hope for the warmer days in between the lingering cold. This March was a particularly sentinel one — Ava arrived. And I was ready to accept her...and as the month has gone on, how quickly I've been able to transition from mourning

Aydin to seeing Aydin in Ava and embracing Ava. Just writing Aydin right now brought tears to my eyes....I miss writing it, hearing my body say it even if just in my mind, but I know it will all be okay. It's so fresh and we've already all adjusted so much. April will be the first full month of her. I look forward to the new month. It will be more than okay.

I was finally starting to feel at peace for more than a day at a time. Early April, one of my longtime best friends, Guita, was set to visit for a weekend with her husband and kids. Guita and I had met on the first day of pediatric residency orientation at the Cleveland Clinic Foundation, and we were inseparable for the next five years. Her husband was a neurosurgery resident while Babak was a general surgery resident, and we saw each other more than we saw our husbands. Our first kids were born within two months of each other, our second kids within three weeks of each other. Our husbands would joke about calling each other and planning when they'd get us pregnant. We had our third kids within ten days of each other. The difference was that when she learned that her second baby was going to be a girl, I was jealous and sad, pregnant with my second "boy." I decided that for my third pregnancy, I'd try to control the outcome.

I read some books on how to have girls, most of which said X sperm swim slower but last longer, whereas Y sperm swim faster but die sooner. So if you wanted to have a girl, you should try to time intercourse three to four days before ovulation. The fast Y sperm would arrive sooner, but there would be no egg to fertilize, and they would die; the hearty, slow X sperm would get there later, when there was an egg. I was skeptical, but there was no harm in taking my temperature every day and trying to predict my ovulation pattern. I filled in Babak on my plan. He rolled his eyes. "Whatever. You just tell me when to show up and do my part, and I'll be there."

During my third pregnancy, I threw up quite a bit and lost some weight before I started gaining, but it was nowhere as bad as the pregnancy with Ava. I didn't need IV fluids at any point. I went to the eighteen-week ultrasound appointment alone because Babak was working. Both Babak and my mom had been with me for the first one, just Babak and I for the second, and here I was by myself for my third. That morning, I gave myself a little pep talk. *This is it. This is the day you find out you're having a third boy. You're going to be a girly-girl momma to three sons, and that's okay.* I just wanted to find out, accept it, and move on.

By this point I had decided there probably was not going to be a fourth child, regardless of the outcome of this ultrasound. I hadn't wanted a girl just so that I could dress her up in little pink dresses and put barrettes in her hair; I wanted to be able to have an adult mother-daughter relationship. I had two sisters. My mom had five. But by this point, I knew how rewarding it was to have sweet little boys. And of course years later, as Armon grew into the most sensitive teenage boy I've ever met, I realized just how rewarding an adult mother-son relationship could be. I wouldn't trade my relationship with him for the world.

When the ultrasound technician told me that she couldn't see a penis or testicles, and that she was fairly sure she was seeing labia, I asked, "Are you sure?" in disbelief. She reiterated that she was fairly certain. She pointed out how labia look almost like hamburger buns and outlined them for me on the screen. A second technician in the room agreed with her. I started crying. They thought I was upset and wanted a boy. I could barely find my voice to say, "No, I wanted a girl. I already have two boys."

"Well then, you go out today and buy every single pink onesie and blanket you can find," she told me.

"But are you sure?"

"Well, if you really can't believe you're having a girl and would feel better, leave the tags on just in case, until she's born."

I called Babak, who was in the operating room. I asked the scrub nurse to take the phone to his ear while he was operating. "It's a girl," I whispered.

"I'm having a girl!" he announced to everyone in the operating room, and I heard them cheering in the background. I then called my mom, still in tears, barely able to form the words "It's a girl" again.

For our third pregnancies, Guita had a boy, and I had Shayda. I spent years thinking that we'd both ended up with two boys and a girl in the end. But, as it turned out, my second pregnancy was also a girl. When Ava first told us she was a girl, I thought it was karmic payback for my ungratefulness and jealousy during my second pregnancy — but then again, the minute Ava was born and I named her Aydin, I fell in love. I was no longer sad to be having a boy. I couldn't blame myself for the thoughts I had before the birth.

Guita's and my kids grew up together during our Cleveland years. Once our family moved to Indianapolis for Babak's fellowship, and later to LA, we still made it a point to get together with Guita's family at least once a year. On every vacation together over the years, the kids quickly fell back into an instant, easy friendship. Now Guita and her family, who lived in Florida, were visiting for one day.

Guita was one of the close friends to whom I had told everything, but Ava did not know that. Guita's kids didn't officially know anything, although they had seen Ava's pictures on Instagram and therefore, like other people who did not officially know, had some clues about the situation. I asked Ava what she wanted to do. They would be in our home, where she was Ava. "What do you want to do while Guita and her kids are here? Do you want me to tell Guita ahead of time that you are a girl and they should call you Ava?"

She thought about it for less than a minute. "No, they're just here for a day. It will be easier if I just go by Aydin, and I'll wear more gender-neutral clothes for that day."

"Are you sure?" I asked. "Her kids follow you on Instagram, so they've obviously seen some changes in you. It's your decision, but it's okay with me if we tell them."

"No," she persisted. "I'm not ready to tell all of them. It will be fine. I'll go by Aydin for a day at home."

When they visited, the four of us adults went out to eat together. I love Guita, and her husband, Caleb, is also an old and good friend, but when we went out to eat, he commented: "I think you guys should wait at least a couple more years before you consider hormones, because teenagers change their minds about things all the time." I knew he had good intentions, but it hurt. Still, they were only visiting for twenty-four hours, so I didn't say anything, and neither did Babak.

When people say these things, do they realize how hard these decisions already are for parents? No parent takes the decision to allow and support their child in their transition lightly. For many, the choice is stark. It is life or death. Do I want a living transitioning child or a suicidal one? There really is no justification for others to give their input or opinion unless they've had actual direct experience with their own child.

Caleb also said, "I'm glad he is just going by Aydin for this weekend, because where we live is conservative. My kids aren't exposed to this type of thing. It would be hard to explain it to them and hard for them to understand." I saw Guita wince when he said it, but she didn't say anything. I didn't want to make her feel worse, so I didn't say anything either. Guita had listened to all my cries and worries over the phone for eighteen years. We changed the subject.

If it had been anyone but Guita's husband, I would have spoken out. I would have said, "I'm sorry if your kids may have a hard time understanding this because of lack of exposure. I'm sorry that you're now going to need to have a conversation with your children explaining what being transgender is, a conversation that you should have had before now, regardless." I would have said, "I'm sorry, but your kids actually probably know what being transgender is, and could probably educate you." And the truth is, those kids would likely not have had a hard time at all. My sister and I had worried about whether my niece would be confused, and she was fine. It is adults who need to take a lesson from kids.

It was good to reconnect, but when they left, I was happy to have Ava go by Ava at home again. After just a few weeks, having her be someone else at home felt like a lie.

At the next Transforming Family meeting, parents were discussing hormones and hormone blockers and their side effects. A couple of parents mentioned that once their male-to-female daughters started estrogen, their hair grew thicker, and their smell changed. They spoke about the change in smell as a good thing, since a teen body on estrogen smells better than a sweaty, testosterone-charged teen body, but I worried. While I don't enjoy the smell of a sweaty teenage boy's room, I didn't want Ava's smell to change.

I started wondering about how Ava would change once she started hormones. I wrote in my journal just a few sentences, worrying that the way she smelled and the feel of her skin would change. I wrote about kissing the back of her neck when I dropped her off at school, inhaling her scent, feeling her skin on my lips. I wrote about how I recognized all my kids by their scent. I put some stars by what I'd written, aware that it was a powerful paragraph that I might come back to one day. Then on April 8, 2018, I ran the Run to Remember half marathon, which pays tribute to first responders and raises funds to support families of those who have fallen. Though I was still running four or five days a week, I hadn't participated in a race for a few months. I didn't run it fast, but it felt good to be coming back to myself a little, whether it was through a few powerful sentences or some slower miles.

A few days later, Shayda's appendix ruptured, and she was hospitalized for almost two weeks. I took off work and dropped 90 percent of the things I would normally have done in order to stay in the hospital with her. Sleeping in a reclining chair next to her bed was exhausting, but this was the most time I'd spent alone with her without other distractions in a long while. I loved just being with her, focusing on her. Waking up with an aching body in the middle of the night, I sat and watched her breathe, asleep in the hospital bed, her hair in two long braids, cheeks gaunt from the weight she'd lost since surgery, the IV in her arm.

I realized that I had missed my little girl. I had been pulled in so many directions over the past year. Part of me was grateful for this reality check, the reminder that all that matters is our health, the forced break. It was a wake-up call that a lot of the running around I was doing every day was not necessary. Fortunately for me, my colleagues took care of all my work while I was gone, fitting my patients into their schedules, and so I didn't need to worry about a pile of work when I got back. But everything else I normally did at home just didn't get done or had to wait.

Repeatedly that year, I was realizing that when forced to simplify, I liked it, I needed it. I didn't have to be a perfectionist or overachiever. I could designate tasks to other people or forgo them. When I left the hospital with Shayda, I continued to say no and turn things down. We had three kids who needed us. The health and safety of all of us was what mattered.

While Shayda was in the hospital, Babak's sister Laila happened to visit. She spent one day sitting with Shayda in the hospital to let me get out for a little. Babak and I went to lunch, and while we were sitting at the bar, we started talking about Ava. Babak looked at his phone, realizing he had not changed her contact name. He had me take a little video of him changing her contact name in his phone from Aydin to Ava, and we sent it to her.

Back home from the hospital, I felt a new appreciation for the nurses and the ancillary staff. I enjoyed being back in my routine of running and going to work, coming home at night and just being with the kids, sipping my glass of malbec, and doing more reading or writing. After going back to the journal entry about Ava's scent, I wrote a piece called "On My Transitioning Teenager: How Do You Record a Scent?" It was short, but I knew it was powerful and would appeal to parents. I submitted it to the *Washington Post*, and two days later, I heard back from the editor of the parenting section. She planned to publish it in a few weeks, and she would pay me for it.

I got a rush from knowing that my writing would be out there again. I decided to donate the two hundred dollars to a trans charity of Ava's choice. We decided on Transforming Family, a place that had made all the difference for us and so many others.

CHAPTER 9

PRESCRIBING *a* NEW STORY

I looked at my reflection in the mirror, trying to see if I still recognized myself. *You can handle this — it's just another day*, I tried to convince the eyes staring back at me from the mirror. Did my eyes still sing and dance with joy, as my late Aunt Shaheen had once said they did? She had been holding my face in between her hands, locking eyes with me in an airport after six years apart. I can still feel her palms on my cheeks.

My dark brown eyes maintained their pain and worry, but I looked away. What had been scheduled months in advance seemed to have suddenly snuck up on me. It was May 2, 2018, the day of our first appointment at the Center for Transyouth Health and Development at the Children's Hospital of Los Angeles, just less than a year since that first call in Thailand, to discuss Ava's medical transition. I wasn't ready, but I knew I might never be. I had to remind myself that what mattered was not my readiness but Ava's body, which was getting more masculinized each day by testosterone that had no respect for anyone's timeline.

Although Babak had taken Ava to only one of her therapy appointments with Dr. Stern, leaving me to handle the rest, he had taken the afternoon off from work for this one. He wanted to be there for her, and for me, and I knew that I would not be able to relay all the information without recording it, or even worse, having him on a speakerphone the whole time. In my own pediatric practice, this is one of my greatest pet peeves. I end up having to repeat half the conversation to the parent on the phone. They can't read my facial expressions, and they can't observe my exam. I was certainly not going to put another physician through that. If you don't think the other parent can reliably relay what transpires at an appointment, then you should be there yourself. I signed Ava out of school early; Babak drove.

We drove mostly in silence. The distance, seven miles, takes about forty-five minutes in LA traffic. Children's Hospital is almost directly across from the Kaiser Permanente hospital on Sunset Boulevard where I gave birth to Shayda, and the drive took me back to that time almost twelve years earlier.

When we moved to Los Angeles, after two years in Indianapolis while Babak completed a plastic surgery fellowship, I was seven months pregnant with Shayda. Seven years after getting married, I was pregnant with my third and last child, a girl, and living in Los Angeles within a couple miles of my aunt's old condominium. All my plans had panned out, check, check, check. I joked that my daughter had been waiting to be born in Hollywood, not in Cleveland like the boys. Although my ultrasound in Indianapolis had confirmed that I was having a girl, a little part of me still worried that the baby was a boy, the penis just tucked and not visible in the image. When I went to my first prenatal appointment at Kaiser Sunset, the obstetrician said, "I'm going to order an ultrasound. We like to have our own ultrasounds on record." I felt relief when this ultrasound confirmed that there was no penis or testicles in sight.

When my contractions started, ten days before my due date, at first I wasn't sure if it was labor. My first two labors had been induced at forty weeks, so no one was expecting Shayda to arrive a little early. As we drove along Sunset, with me writhing in pain and now 100 percent sure this was labor, I was excited that I was finally going to be a mother to a daughter.

As it turned out, Shayda was born by emergency C-section. I had started bleeding from a placental abruption (a complication in which the placenta separates early from the uterus), and the baby's heart rate had been undetectable. The anesthesiologist had completely knocked me out for the surgery. The first incision was made at 10:02 a.m.; Shayda was out at 10:03 a.m. A couple of hours later, when I was waking up from anesthesia, before I could even open my eyes, I heard Babak's voice beside me and muttered, "It's a girl, right?"

Now, as we parked just across from Kaiser, it felt like going to some sort of prenatal or birth appointment for Ava. Once again I blamed myself for my stupidity in caring about whether I had boys or girls. We were going to talk about blocking her body's testosterone and starting her on estrogen. Was Ava actually my first girl, or was Shayda my first girl? I thought of Shayda as my first daughter, but would there come a day when that narrative would finally change in my mind, when I would think of Ava as my first? Did it matter? Would Shayda's story and history change because of Ava? And what if it did?

Shayda was born on my late Aunt Shaheen's birthday. She was the aunt I was closest to growing up, the aunt whose unexpected early death had made me realize on my runs that I needed to live my life to the fullest and start taking risks — check everything off my bucket list. She was the aunt whose death had made me want to never visit Iran again, afraid that I'd step off the plane and not be able to breathe when I didn't see her eyes scanning the passengers for me. She'd had two boys and then a girl. I got pregnant with Shayda about a year after her death.

Shayda's early arrival on Shaheen's birthday had felt like a gift and a sign from the universe, from my aunt, finally making me a mother to a daughter. I'd spent a lifetime creating different narratives and stories like this. Now, all the stories that I'd concocted in my head were being questioned, but did any of it matter? Stories are made up. They can be rewritten. The ending could be happy or sad, depending on the spin I chose to put on it. I could rewrite these stories, or I could stop giving them so much power.

We got out of the car and rode the elevator in silence. The thumping in my heart was so loud, I felt it should be audible to others without a stethoscope. The security guard outside the clinic gave us each a visitor sticker. I don't remember how I signed Ava in, but most likely, I wrote "Ava (Aydin)."

The first appointment involved meeting with the center's social worker. A woman with a short, punkish hairstyle called the three of us into her office. She had her ID on a lanyard around her neck, with a pin on the ribbon that said "she." I later noticed that all her emails to me also ended with the signature "Sage, she/her." All the emails from the center specified the sender's preferred pronouns, although it didn't seem like any of the people sending the emails were trans. It was just a reminder that we shouldn't assume anyone's pronouns, and that we should all tell people our pronouns. I liked it.

Sage gathered some background information on us, told us about the services the center provided, and asked if there was anything we needed help with other than the medical issues, which would be addressed by the doctor. I asked if there were any other social opportunities, other than Transforming Family, for Ava to meet people and make friends. "Ava does have several good friends who are cisgender girls, but it would be nice for her to have more trans friends who understand what she is going through." It was the first time I had used the term *cisgender girls*, and I thought, *Who am I, using this lingo that I didn't even know anything about not that long ago?* A cisgender person is someone whose gender identity matches the sex they were assigned at birth based on their genitalia. So, since I identify as a woman and was born with a vagina and declared a girl, I am cisgender. On the car ride home, I asked Ava proudly, "Did you notice me use the term *cisgender girls?*"

"Yes, I did. Impressive," Ava replied.

Sage gave us the names of a couple of other support groups that met in the teen center at Children's Hospital. Neither met at a time or location that Ava could commute to by herself. Sage also asked if Ava wanted to speak with her by herself. Ava said no. "There is nothing my parents don't know about." We then left Sage's office and waited to meet Ava's doctor, Dr. James Carlson.

We sat around a small table in his office, Ava between Babak and me, Dr. Carlson across from Ava. He looked to be in his fifties, with warm brown eyes and a gentle voice and demeanor. Children's Hospital uses electronic medical records, like almost every other health system now, but for that first visit, he did not take notes on the computer. He started by asking Ava, "How did you guys end up here today?"

Ava gave him a chronological account of events, which started with her having questions about sexuality at the age of twelve. Dr. Carlson listened without interrupting and nodded his head and said, "That sounds like a very typical story that I hear."

Part of me still expected that he might say something like, "Oh, so this is all new and just about a year old, so let's see how things evolve over time," but he did not. He did ask if Ava had a therapist. We said she had been working with Dr. Nathaniel Stern for a few months. "I signed some release forms with Dr. Stern, so you can communicate with him regarding Ava," I volunteered.

"Nate, Dr. Stern, he's great," Dr. Carlson smiled in response. I don't think he ever contacted him, but maybe knowing that she was with the right therapist did help him feel comfortable that this was not a phase for Ava, and maybe it didn't. Maybe he had heard so many postpuberty stories like Ava's that he could be virtually certain that Ava was trans. Maybe if Ava had not been with a therapist he knew, or even had a therapist at all, Dr. Carlson would still have felt confident that Ava was trans just from his own experience. (Later I would find out that having a therapist is not a requirement for proceeding with a medical transition.) He did say,

"I'm always happy when I get to sit down with a family, both parents on the same page, everyone there to support the child." I felt good and guilty at the same time. *You have no idea how much I've already fucked this up.*

He hardly wrote anything on his notepad, although we met with him for over an hour. I made sure he understood my big concern, that this still might just be a phase. "I'm just worried that we'll start hormones and she'll change her mind later."

"When a child presents after already starting puberty, the chance that they will change their mind is only 2 to 3 percent," he told me. "I've been treating trans kids since the nineties, about twenty years. Sometimes kids who when they are very young seem trans will change and not be trans around age seven or eight or early puberty, but once they start puberty and they say they are trans, they are."

Then he turned to Ava and said, "If we start hormones and it doesn't feel right and you decide you are not ready for this or you are not sure about this, you just tell us, and we stop. I won't be upset, and your parents won't be upset. You just tell us, and we stop." He made it seem like it was no big deal. I know that he was trying to convey to her that we were relying on her to tell us how she felt and that it would be okay to change her mind — the door was always open for that as well. I appreciated that. I didn't want Ava to be scared to come to me in the future if she did change her mind.

Dr. Carlson always looked directly at Ava while talking to her and treated her as a girl. He spoke to her seeing her. I felt very comfortable and at ease with him, just as I had felt with Dr. Stern. Looking around his office, I noticed pictures of what I guessed to be adolescent daughters. I concluded he was probably a heterosexual, cisgender male with daughters, someone who cared about treating kids, not, as part of me feared, a transgender person with a "trans agenda," someone who would push for Ava's medical transition out of ulterior motives.

I write these sentences knowing how ridiculous and faulty my thinking was. I am now a pediatrician with a trans child who is learning more about treating trans kids, both to educate myself and also to prepare me if I want to get involved in treating trans kids one day. So, by my own definition, I am someone with a trans agenda. But of course I would never rush to put a child on hormones or try to push preconceived ideas about gender identity. My only agenda is to make sure that a child is seen as a whole person and treated appropriately. I would never try to make a cisgender person trans, or a transgender person cis, nor would I ever think I would have the power to do so.

No one can make a cisgender person trans.

No one can make a transgender person cis.

But I record these thoughts that I am ashamed to acknowledge because they are the truth, and because if I have thought them, then there are likely other parents of trans kids who may be thinking them, too.

Dr. Carlson went over the different options for blocking Ava's testosterone — a histrelin implant or the medication spironolactone. The histrelin implant, he explained, had fewer side effects than spironolactone and would last for two to three years, and we should be able to get insurance authorization for it because Ava was under sixteen. Most insurance companies cover the cost of histrelin for children, since it has fewer side effects than other treatment options, but those sixteen and older are treated as adults for insurance coverage purposes. (Bicalutamide, another oral antiandrogen, is now being increasingly used instead of spironolactone in older teens and adults because it has fewer side effects, but this was not an option at the time Ava was being seen.) He also reviewed the risks and benefits of starting estrogen.

He also said that if we wanted to freeze Ava's sperm to enable her to have biological children in the future, this was the time to do it. "If you don't freeze sperm now, the chance that she'll want to come off hormones later for at least six months to start making sperm again is very low. Most people don't do that, not wanting to remasculinize."

On that visit, he did not do a physical exam, and we did not leave his little circular table. "I use the first visit to give you all the information you need. If after digesting all the information, you want to proceed with hormone therapy, then you schedule a follow-up visit for a physical exam and hormone initiation. I find doing an exam on the first visit with kids who do not feel comfortable in their body a little invasive. I want them to first decide if they are comfortable with me and come back ready for the exam."

This timeline came as a surprise to me. He wasn't going to make her wait a couple of years to start hormones, as I had initially declared with certainty to Ava. He was going to make her wait just one visit. I hadn't known anything about transgender care.

Like Sage, Dr. Carlson asked Ava if she would like to talk with him in private, and she said no. Once again, it was nice to know that we were in on everything, that she didn't feel like there was anything she couldn't tell us. I recalled both Hope and Dr. Stern telling me that I should feel good that we were among the first people Ava came out to, because many trans kids tell most of their friends before telling their parents.

Dr. Carlson also went over the changes to expect with starting hormones, such as redistribution of fat and some breast development. He went over possible future surgeries, such as facial feminization and vaginoplasty, and Ava said that she did want vaginoplasty at some point. "Well, a lot of people who think they want vaginoplasty later decide that they don't," Dr. Carlson commented. "Because being a woman is up here, in your brain and mind. For a lot of people, once they are on hormones and get some electrolysis and are 'passing,' they decide not to have vaginoplasty. You have a long time ahead of you to see what you decide."

Passing was a term that we did not associate with the transgender community at that time. We knew of the term's historical association with racial discrimination, when light-skinned African Americans were described as being able to "pass" as white, but in the transgender community, it refers to a transgender person moving through the world as themselves, with people assuming they are cisgender, not trans. Passing was something Ava said she aspired to at that time, and I imagine that many other trans people likely desire the same, although I can't speak for them. I liked Dr. Carlson's repeated emphasis on the view that being a woman is in your brain and not your genitals. I could have a mastectomy and shave my head, but I would still know that I was a woman — I would feel it in my core. I don't know if Ava will change her mind about vaginoplasty, but I liked his assurance that she already was a woman.

During our meeting with Sage, she had gone over the process of a legal name change. She strongly advised that we consider changing Ava's legal name before she took the Scholastic Aptitude Test. "For some reason, it is really hard to get the name changed on SAT score reports, so if you're planning on getting a legal name change before college, it's best to do it before even taking the SATs to make the entire college application process much easier." Given that Ava was only a freshman in high school, we still had some time.

It was amazing how fast everything progressed after that first appointment. We made a follow-up appointment for three weeks later, on May 24, 2018, exactly one year to the day after the Thailand call. Although getting an initial appointment at the center had taken months, once Ava was in the system, follow-up appointments were easy to get, and the support and communication were excellent.

When we left, I knew that the first order of business was to freeze her sperm. I remembered her expressing a desire to be a parent as early as when she was ten, and I didn't want her saying to me in twenty years that I hadn't preserved her ability to have biological children. I wanted to be able to one day say, "I did everything I could for you," whether or not her sperm was ever used. I started investigating options right away. There was a sperm bank in Westwood, not too far from us, but its reviews on Yelp were not great, and it was open only during school hours. I didn't want to pull Ava out of school for this. I emailed Sage, who suggested a sperm bank on the other side of the country that allowed users to collect samples at home and FedEx them to their location. I thought to myself, *Great, she won't have to miss school, I don't have to drive her somewhere in LA traffic.... This should be perfect.* I had no idea what I was getting myself into.

I called the sperm bank on a Saturday morning. A woman with a sweet voice answered. I explained the situation to her, and she described the process. I could hear what sounded like a baby starting to stir and make noise in the background, and then I was 99 percent sure she was nursing a baby while talking to me — the suck and gulp, I've heard it thousands of times, having nursed three kids and witnessed hundreds of mothers nurse their babies in my office. I wondered if this was some type of mom-and-pop sperm bank to which we would be entrusting Ava's sperm for twenty years or more, but then I talked myself down. It was a Saturday, after all; the lab was closed on Saturdays, and she was just answering the phone. And the thought of a mother at the other end of the line was also comforting. *She understands*, I thought. *She'd do the same for her child, whatever it takes.*

She informed me that Ava's sperm count was likely to be highest if we collected samples every three days, with no expelling of sperm in between. Further, since the lab could receive samples only Monday through Thursday, I had to put Ava on an every-third-day masturbation schedule. If the third day was a Monday, Tuesday, or Wednesday, I'd rush the sample to FedEx. If the third day was any other day, we'd discard it. Also, we needed to collect the sample just before FedEx's last shipping deadline, because it had to reach the lab within eighteen hours. And I'd have to mix the semen with a solution that helped keep it viable for the shipment across the US.

What the literal fuck?

This was *not* what I signed up for when I decided to have kids. Never, ever, in any of my visions of myself as a mother had I expected that one day I'd be ironing my "son's" dress, much less collecting semen from my child's strictly scheduled masturbation sessions and taking it to the FedEx office. Again I talked myself down. *There are parents who do this with their teens before they start chemotherapy for leukemia. Your child is healthy. Stop being so angry. Be grateful. Would you rather she had leukemia?*

Well, actually, yes. As horrible as it sounds, there were many times just a couple of months before, when I was trying to decide whether or not to let Ava proceed with hormones, when I had thought that our choices would be easier if she had leukemia. When a child has leukemia, there is a chemotherapy protocol, and you follow it. When a child says she's trans, but you are not sure if she is really trans or it's just a phase or what, ultimately you have to decide if you are going to stop your child's puberty. Are you going to alter their ability to ever have biological children?

I know it seems heartless, but sometimes I felt it would be easier to be told exactly what I had to do to treat my child's life-threatening illness than to make life-altering decisions I wasn't sure about. Of course, it's not that simple. Sometimes parents of children with cancer have to make hard decisions about treatment with limited information and no guarantees. Some cancer medications have severe and potentially fatal side effects. I know that I should not have been comparing having a trans child to having a child with cancer, but these were my thoughts, and I have to own them and be honest about them.

To add to my woes, since Babak got home from work later than I did, I would be the one, yet again, who would have to deal with the sperm banking. I would have to rush home and mix the sperm with the preservative and drop it off at FedEx just before their last pickup, then track the shipment on my computer. Back when we were dating and I told Babak that eventually I'd want to work part time to spend more time with the kids, this was not what I had in mind. Now I told Babak, "I should not be the one who is handling her sperm. You should be doing this."

"She's a girl now. Bodily functions are mother-daughter territory and not my job," Babak responded. He was trying to inject some humor into the situation. He just wouldn't be at home during the window of sperm collection and delivery, otherwise he would have helped.

The first time we were ready to collect a semen sample was on a Monday. I had explained the process to Ava the week before. "So this means that to get the best sample, I need you to discard a sample on Friday afternoon, then not do anything that would discard anything between then and Monday afternoon, then give me a sample right after school. Do you understand what that actually means?" I was trying to avoid using the terms *masturbation*, *semen*, and *ejaculation*, despite being a pediatrician who was comfortable talking to other teens using all of those terms.

"Yes, Mom, I know exactly what that means," Ava responded.

"So do you think that's something you can do?"

"Yes."

Midafternoon on the previous Friday, I had sent her a reminder text that it was "time to discard" and followed up an hour later to make sure she had done it. That following Monday, I picked her up from school, we rushed home, and I sent her to the bathroom while I waited in my room. I was in disbelief that I knew exactly what was happening in her bathroom. I wasn't thinking about future grandchildren, but just trying to distract myself and not look at my watch to see how long it was taking. Then I heard her door open, and she came to my room and handed me the cup. I felt its warmth in my palm. I took it to my bathroom and opened it with shaking hands. *Don't breathe*, I told myself. *Don't let yourself smell it.* I was continually exhaling through my nostrils as if I were doing some weird breath-work exercise in yoga class in an effort to avoid inhaling. I mixed in the sperm preserver, tightened the lid, and finally took a big breath. I put the cup in the FedEx bag and jumped in my car. At FedEx, the counter person told me, "Those types of packages you can just put in the box outside."

"This has to go out tonight. You said on the phone your last ship-out is at 5 p.m., but I don't want this in a box in the sun for fifteen minutes until pickup."

She looked at me suspiciously. "Fine, I'll take it," she said.

"But you'll make sure it goes out with the pickup tonight?"

"Yes, you should be able to track it on the computer by 5:15."

Back home, I checked my computer at 5:15. It had been picked up. *There, that wasn't terrible*, I say to myself. *You only have to do that two more times.* I tracked the package until it arrived at the lab the next day.

For the sperm banking, Ava was required to have a series of blood tests, including an HIV test and a hepatitis C test. There was no way around it. I asked Ava's pediatrician to put in the order for the tests, and I took Ava to the lab in our office building on a Saturday morning. She was nervous and looked pale. Sitting in the chair after her blood draw, she looked even paler, but they needed to call in the next patient. I found a piece of hard candy and gave it to her, hoping the sugar would make her feel better. Leaving the elevator, she was as white as a ghost. "Spit out the candy!" I yelled at her, afraid that she would faint and choke on it. She spat it out, and two seconds later she fainted in the parking lot. She was too big and heavy for me to stop her from falling to the ground. I merely broke her fall so her head didn't hit the cement.

I sat with her on the ground until she came to and was feeling well enough to stand up and walk to the car. No one passed by to help us. I worried about how the hell she could possibly have a vaginoplasty if she fainted after a blood draw. I would not be able to help her with the complicated aftercare of a vaginoplasty. That, I decided, was where I was going to draw the line. We got home and I called Babak, angry at him once again.

Later that day, I checked in on Ava in her bedroom. She was lying on her bed in a white tank shirt and a long, flowy black skirt, her face turned away from me. Her hair was getting longer. I saw a girl lying on the bed. I stopped breathing. Although I'd been using all female pronouns for Ava for two months, in my head I still didn't think of her as a girl all the time. But at that moment, what I saw was a girl taking a nap. I quietly took a picture, closed the door, and sent the picture to my sisters. I told myself to calm down. *Maybe she'll never have a vaginoplasty. And if she ever does, I'm not going to worry about the aftercare now.*

Paria finds Ava napping and is caught by surprise
that she looks like a girl lying on a bed.

Soon after this came the school's end-of-year choir concert. Ava was in the men's choir. Although she had been given the option of wearing the women's choir dress, during some of the songs, standing among all the other boys in men's choir, she would have been the only choir member onstage in a dress, and she decided that she would rather just wear the men's clothing before switching to a dress for sophomore year.

Babak and I looked at Ava on the stage in her men's white shirt, black pants, black tie, belt, and men's shoes. "You know, this is the last time we're going to see her in men's clothes," Babak said to me.

"I know. I've been thinking about that. I'm happy it's the last time," I said. It didn't look like my child standing up there anymore. It seemed like my child not being herself, forced to wear a costume she didn't like. I didn't feel sad about it. I knew how uncomfortable I felt when I wore something that didn't fit my body right. I couldn't imagine how uncomfortable it must feel to be wearing clothing that caused you to be completely misgendered, clothes that felt like an erasure of who you are — a lie. And I knew that after that night, we wouldn't need those clothes anymore. They could be donated to Goodwill, because they would be too tight for Armon, and Ava would never wear them again.

Our nineteenth wedding anniversary was on May 22, 2018. My heart felt heavy. All I wanted to do was cry. I wrote in my diary:

> Just when you think you've accepted something, grief sneaks up on you like a tidal wave and knocks you over, out of the blue. Maybe it's because you've been avoiding the wave all together. Maybe if you had regularly ventured out, allowing the little waves to just carry you with a little blip of grief, or just even dipped your toes in periodically...maybe if you would allow yourself to regularly pause and feel, rather than avoid and go, the tidal wave of grief wouldn't have to crash over you...making you feel paralyzed for a few days before you could get up again. Maybe one day you'll learn to just phase and feel — to dip your toes in every day.

I guess I wrote this because since my talk with Dr. Stern, when he confirmed that Ava was a girl, my mindset had been "Move forward as fast as you can." I had busied myself with all the appointments for transitioning, and I had also been trying my best to start seeing Ava as my daughter. Although I still cried in the car at times, I hadn't allowed myself to go back to really grieving. It had just hit me like a tidal wave that day. Babak and I went out to dinner, and I tried my best to not let my grief show.

I missed my baby boy — I missed my vision of the handsome man that boy would have become. I told Babak, "I'm never going to know what an adult version of Aydin would have been like. I just can't seem to get over that."

"You *do* know," he said. "An adult version of Aydin would have been either a depressed and isolated person, or dead. But the real adult version of Aydin is Ava, and she will be happy and thriving and surrounded with friends." He was right. I knew he was right. I would remind myself of that every time these thoughts recurred. I would tell myself, *Your child will get to be an adult and not join the staggering statistics of unsupported transgender teens who commit suicide.*

A couple of days later, on May 24, Ava and I were back at Children's Hospital for our follow-up appointment with Dr. Carlson. For this second visit, Dr. Carlson wanted to talk to Ava alone and do a physical exam as well. When I see teenage patients, I often ask to speak to them alone, so I could imagine what their conversation was about. He was probably asking her about sexual activity, alcohol, marijuana, and recreational drugs. But I thought to myself, *I hope you are also telling her that just because she is trans, she should never compromise for love or affection, that she should never settle for less than she wants because of her body not being like that of other girls. I hope you are telling her to never stay in a situation in which she is not comfortable, to know that she should always be safe — never taken advantage of…to never ever settle or allow someone to make her feel less than….* I knew these were conversations that I should have been having with her myself. I once asked Dr. Stern to discuss these things with her, and he told me, "I can do that, but you should be doing that as well."

That day we were given Ava's first prescription for estrogen: estradiol, two milligrams per day. We were still waiting for insurance authorization for the testosterone blocker — that would take a few more months — so the estrogen would have very little effect, but still, she was happy to be getting the prescription. After receiving the sperm analysis from the lab on the East Coast, we had decided to go ahead and store some sperm at the sperm bank in Westwood as well. We were going to finish that process over the next couple of weeks, and then she could start taking the estrogen.

Exactly one year to the day from when we first got that phone call in

Thailand, Ava had her estrogen in hand. It seemed crazy. We had initially told her that she needed to be in therapy for at least a couple of years before she could start hormones, and that we wouldn't even consider it until she was an adult. Looking back, I knew that was ridiculous. There was no way she would have lasted that long. Still, I had thought hormones would be at least a couple of years off, that we would wait long enough to see if this was just another phase. But once we started, there was no slowing down or stopping. It wasn't that we didn't have the choice: slowing down just wasn't the right thing to do. The right thing to do was to treat and parent the child who was in front of us and, to a certain degree, hand over the control and responsibility to the experts, her doctor and therapist in this field, who agreed that the time was right. Relinquishing the worry about whether I was doing the wrong thing made things a little easier on me.

On May 25, 2018, my piece "On My Transitioning Teenager: How Do You Record a Scent?" got published in the *Washington Post*. Ava was not out yet, but school was ending within a week, and she was going to start her summer health class as Ava. I posted the piece on my Twitter account. I had a pretty small following, but the response from that small group of people was incredible. The comments included:

"Beautiful, honest, and loving piece. Thank you for sharing."

"Beautiful piece. Thank you for the reminder to slow down and breathe in my children before it's too late. Wishing your family lots of love."

"PERFECTION."

"Hugs, hugs, and more hugs, from one mom going through the same thing. I never thought of their smell, but I am sorry I neglected to record their voice."

It felt good to have finally put it out there, even though I had never felt I was actively trying to hide anything. It felt good to have my writing get a response, to have it move people. Of course, the *Washington Post* put it on their own Twitter feed, and there was some insensitive and ridiculous commentary from Twitter trolls, but I was expecting that, and it only confirmed that more of our stories need to be out in the world, until one day being transgender is finally normalized for everyone. I know that day is coming. I don't know when, but it is coming.

Over Memorial Day weekend, Juliet came over with her kids. Ava was ready to come out to Mila and Jackson. I had Juliet tell Jackson before they came over, since Ava didn't want to have the conversation with him herself for some reason, or have it happen in front of her. They came over, called her Ava, and used female pronouns. They didn't miss a beat. Nothing seemed any different with Jackson and Ava: they headed off to her room as they had done for years.

Ava had already created a Facebook account for her Madrigals choir group and listed her gender as female despite not being officially out. The last day of school was May 31. I couldn't wait, because after that day, I'd just be able to tell anyone new that I met, "I have two daughters and a son." I was glad that this in-between phase, with Ava identifying with one gender and identity at home and with select people, and another one in public, was about to end. We only had to live that way for a few months, but some families do it for years until their child is ready to come out to everyone. I don't know how they handle that. It takes a toll — at least it did on me, the truth teller and sharer of everything.

After school was out, I took Ava to her first appointment at the Westwood sperm bank. While I signed her in, I noticed cartoon sperm magnets all over the receptionist's desk. In the waiting room, I decided to have a conversation with Ava on an issue that had been weighing me down. "I need you to know that although we are freezing your sperm, there is no guarantee about the viability of your sperm twenty years from now. And even though we are storing some at two different sperm banks, it may still not end up being enough for you to have biological kids, even if the sperm are viable twenty years from now. I need to know that you understand that we can't guarantee you can have future biological children before you start your estrogen."

"I know that, Mom," she responded. "But I also know that I will be a mom one day. Whether this way or another, I'm going to be a mom."

She used the word *mom* and not *parent*. This wasn't the first time. She was so sure. Her certainty about seeing herself as a mother was reassuring for me.

I am a woman, I will always be in women's roles.

How was it that she was more sure of who she was at fourteen than I had ever been about myself in my entire life? I was so proud of her. To see her know and believe and not even question that she would have a partner and coparent one day was reassuring and inspiring and awe-inducing. I breathed a sigh of relief.

I recalled another conversation we had had about children, driving home after a therapy session with Dr. Stern. Ava told me that she might end up in a relationship with an American and not an Iranian one day. "That's fine," I said. "That's what I've been assuming would happen with all three of you, that it is more likely that you would end up with a non-Iranian than an Iranian. Just because your dad and I married each other doesn't mean I think that's what is going to happen with my kids. It doesn't matter to me who you guys end up with as long as it is a good person, and you don't even have to all get married. I just want you all to be happy. It doesn't have to be with someone, but if it is with someone, it just has to be a good person."

Then she said, "And you know, I may have to end up adopting one day."

"That's fine," I said.

"And it may end up having to be a girl from Asia or something."

I told her that was fine, too — that it didn't matter to me whether my kids adopted or not, that all my grandchildren would be the same to me, biological or adopted, American or not. She was happy with that. Maybe it was just that we had such a hard time accepting her as a girl in the first place that made her think I might react negatively, but all I really want for my children is for them to be happy and fulfilled.

The waiting room door opened, bringing me back to the present. A young, petite blonde technician poked her head in and asked us to come into her office. She went over some paperwork and procedures. She also told us that under California law the bank needed blood work done within a month of the semen storage date, which meant getting another set of blood tests. When it was time for Ava to get a cup and give her sample, the technician addressed me: "Mom, there are some magazines in the room that help some people produce a sample. Given Ava is fourteen and a minor, I can remove them or leave them." I told her that it was okay to leave them, and Ava could decide whether to use them. I found it cute that she asked me. Ava thought everyone at the sperm bank was sensitive and sweet. That's part of their job. But it made me sad that anytime someone was pleasant to her and just made her feel like a regular girl and human being, she thought it was special.

Ava's self-assuredness about being a woman and a mother one day, combined with a series of questions she started asking me once she realized we were going to let her start hormone therapy, got me thinking about myself. Her first question was, "How long do you think I need to be on estrogen before I start getting some breast tissue?" I thought about my breasts, how much I complain about their sagging, and how many times they have been squished into x-ray machines for mammograms. I remembered the ultrasound appointment to check on a suspicious area of breast tissue, followed by the two-hour MRI to further check that same spot. I thought about all the clothes that I would like to wear but can't because they'd look better with no bra or a strapless bra, and I am past that phase of my life. I recalled all the times I had had negative thoughts about my breasts, while Ava was eagerly waiting for the day when she'd have breasts, as some proof or validation of her identity as a woman.

Another day, she asked me, "You know how girls have thighs that are wider at the top? Do you think there are any exercises I can do to make mine look wider?" I'd found her taking my ten-pound weights into her room, doing exercises from YouTube videos to build up her glutes. I thought about how much I have always hated my hips and thighs. My mom, her five sisters, and I all have the same wide, "childbearing" hips. I have cropped them out of pictures or been frustrated by the way I look in pants. Until I became a runner, I yo-yo dieted my entire life, trying to change my body shape. I never succeeded. And here Ava was hoping and waiting for the day when estrogen would redistribute weight to her thighs and hips, giving her the hourglass shape that has traditionally defined a woman. I love being a woman, so why had I always hated the curves of my very womanly figure?

Although I'd already given up dieting and trying to lose those last extra pounds, I was still often frustrated when trying on clothes. But one day, trying on a cute off-white dress, I stepped back and looked at myself in the dressing room mirror. Turning to the side, I saw the way the dress clung just a little too much over my hips, and the lines caused by my underwear showing over the little bulge of my abdomen. For the first time, I didn't feel frustrated by what I saw. I just took off the dress, handed it to the salesperson, and said, "Thanks. It didn't work out." I wasn't mad at my body, or the dress. I was grateful for my body and ashamed that it had taken having a trans daughter to make me feel that way. I knew that I would never again be critical of my hips or frustrated by clothes that didn't fit well.

"Your skin is so soft, Mom. Do you think the estrogen will make my skin soft?" Why had I always fought being soft? I thought of all the times when I was young and hugged my mom, burying myself in her soft body, inhaling her scent. I'm going to be okay with being soft, I decided.

In the days leading up to Ava's giving her final semen specimen for storage, I found myself tearing up and feeling emotional again. She would start her estrogen the same night. Ava was excited; she felt like she had been waiting so long. I felt like everything was moving fast and out of my control, but I knew it had to happen. I didn't let her see me cry.

She started estrogen on June 7, 2018. Babak bought a cake and wrote on it, "Congrats Ava on the beginning of your journey." We took pictures, and Ava was beaming and beautiful in them. When you saw how happy she was, you couldn't help being happy for her. But I secretly cried in bed, or in the shower, or in the car.

Babak gets Ava a cake to celebrate starting estrogen
and hormone therapy, June 2018.

I woke up to the news that Anthony Bourdain, the TV celebrity and traveling chef, had committed suicide. Babak and I watched his show regularly, and sometimes the kids saw part of an episode with us. When Bourdain did an episode on traveling to Iran, we made it a point to watch the entire episode as a family. Apart from their contact with relatives in the US, that show, and Rick Steves's TV special on Iran, were the only exposure the kids had had to the culture and heritage of their beautiful country of origin, the generosity and spirit of the people living in Iran who do not represent the government. "These are the real people in Iran," we told them. "This is the country where your grandparents grew up and so much of your extended family still lives."

Babak had been keen to take the kids on a trip to Iran, but I had insisted that we wait until they were older and would appreciate it more. Once Ava came out as bisexual, we had thought it was probably not safe to take them, and the argument was put to rest. Through these shows, we had shown them Iran. Now, learning that Bourdain had taken his own life, I was worried that one of my kids or even Babak would hurt themselves one day. Even with all the emotional ups and downs I'd experienced over the last year, I couldn't imagine ever feeling depressed enough to try to hurt myself. I wondered what type of loneliness he had experienced, what sort of feelings he had been holding in. I gathered my kids and hugged them and told them that in this family, we weren't going to hold any of our feelings in.

CHAPTER 10

OUT *and* PROUD

I was wearing an Old Navy shirt with a little rainbow heart on it and a Pride baseball cap from Target. Babak wore a fedora with a rainbow ribbon and a rainbow wristband. Ava wore an olive-green skirt with a "Love Wins" shirt and a "She" pin. She wore a deep red-maroon lipstick and a barrette in her hair. She was beaming and excited. We were on our way to the Los Angeles Pride Parade on June 10, 2018.

The only other time we'd been to Pride was two years earlier, before Ava had told us anything about her sexuality or gender. The parade coincidentally fell on the day after the mass shooting in which forty-nine people died in a gay bar in Orlando, Florida. We were heartbroken because it was another shooting, another American tragedy, and we had gay friends who were full of love and had enriched our lives. The five of us had gone to the parade as a family, feeling it was the only thing we could do to support the community and wanting to show our kids what love, acceptance, and pride looked like. "I don't understand what they're celebrating," Shayda had said. We'd explained a little bit about the history of the LGBT community and told her that gay marriage had become legal just one year earlier.

Now, two years later, we were going again. Shayda and Armon were both busy, so Babak, Ava, and I were meeting a big group from Trans-forming Family and walking in the parade with them. To be in the parade rather than just a spectator, you have to be part of a recognized group. We met with the Transforming Family group, and they gave us little trans pride flags — pink, blue, and white — to carry with us. Again we took some pictures, and Ava looked happy in all of them. While we were wait-ing to start, we talked to other families. Everyone was proud and sup-portive. When the parade finally started, Babak and I walked with Ava between us. The energy of the crowd was magnificent.

Babak, Ava, and Paria at the LA Pride Parade, June 2018; Ava is out.

That day I posted a picture of the three of us in our rainbow gear, with our trans pride flags and Ava's "She" pin, on my Instagram feed and Facebook page. I added the caption, "Well, we had to wait over 2 hours in the heat before we could get started, but it was well worth getting to walk the entire Pride Parade with our baby #lapride #familyiseverything."

The response from our family and friends, even if they didn't officially know about Ava, was overwhelmingly positive. That night, Ava also posted a series of pictures from the parade on her Instagram feed. She had already erased all her old pictures on Instagram, leaving only a few meme posts. When I first noticed she had done it, a few months back, I was upset. *You can't erase your past*, I thought. *It was still you.* I tried to ask her why she had erased them. All she said was that she didn't want them up. On this day, she erased all her earlier posts, starting her Instagram afresh with pictures from Pride and her being out. The only thing that remained from her old account was a quote from an American musician and comedian that she had attached on her profile page the year before: "'You have to be scared first to have courage; otherwise it wouldn't be courage! Yeah, otherwise you'd just be doing shit.' Daniel Avidan, 2017."

The next day, Ava started health class in summer school. When the teacher called the roll, she said that she went by Ava and not Aydin. She was officially Ava to everyone. When I asked her how her first day had gone, she said that one freshman boy who recognized her from before kept staring at her and then said, "What's wrong with you?" But her friend Gavin had quickly come up and told the boy to leave her alone, and that was it. Otherwise, the day had gone fine. It was done: she was out everywhere. I felt a huge weight had been lifted off my chest. I can't imagine what Ava felt.

On Father's Day, my parents came over. When Ava wished my dad a happy Father's Day, he replied, "Happy granddaughter's day to you." She smiled hugely at the acknowledgment. I got teary-eyed. I think it was the first time that he'd addressed her as a girl, even though he had been supportive from the start. My mom went through an in-between phase when she didn't call her Aydin but addressed her as "honey" instead, but she started calling her Ava within a couple of weeks. She does insist on pronouncing it the Farsi way (Á-va), which is fine with me. After all, I'm the one who wanted Ava to have a name that Iranians use as well.

I started thinking about writing Ava's story and submitting a piece to *Expressing Motherhood*, a Los Angeles theater show in which motherhood stories are shared onstage. I wanted to write, and I wanted there to be more stories about trans kids who present in adolescence, for mothers like me to find in the media when they need to hear them. What Cybele did for me in her Moth video, I wanted to be able to do for someone else one day.

A couple of days later, flowers were delivered to our house from one of my dad's oldest friends from Iran, my Amoo Reza, who is now in his seventies and lives in the Washington, DC, area. They were friends in grade school in Iran and then both moved to the US and continued their friendship here. I grew up with his kids, both in Iran and later in the US and called him by "amoo," or uncle. The flowers were addressed to Ava, the first mail or package she had received in her new name. The card said, "Ava, we love you and support you. We are so proud of you! Lots of love."

I was a mess of tears. Obviously, he was doing this for me, since he had only met Ava a handful of times and not seen her in years, telling me it was okay. And he was doing it for my dad, for both my parents. I had been worried about how my parents would handle questions from their friends. I knew that this friend in particular would be fine, but it was nice for him to have taken the initiative and say, "We're here for all of you, and it's okay." I called him and cried. He shared some memories he had of me in Iran when he used to drive us to school along with his kids, and how we joked and laughed in the car. We each ended the phone call with a simple "I love you."

Waves of emotions were hitting me again. I was both grateful and sad. I missed my son, even though I knew that Aydin and Ava were the same person, that no one had died. My brain understood this, but my heart had not caught up with my brain. I felt I wasn't allowed to say I missed my son. I still feel that way. Whenever I'm in my car by myself, I allow myself to miss him. I close the car door, take a breath, and turn on the ignition, and the tears flow. I get to my destination, pull down the mirror, wipe my eyes, fix my mascara, and take another big breath. I wrote in my journal:

> My greatest challenge is with Ava now. Learning that I have not lost Aydin — that Aydin is here but is just Ava — that on some level, she has always been Ava. That if my child can have such confidence and put herself out there in the world like that, I need to get over my shit. She is teaching me about love and being open — strength — seeing people as beautiful humans. And what I really need to learn here is to let go of fear — fear that her life will be difficult — fear that she won't find the best life partner and will have to compromise — fear that she will get hurt or beat up — fear that she won't have the best life possible just because of this. It's time to learn to let fear go — to lead with love.

A few days later, more mail arrived, this time delivering something I had ordered, a replacement for a Share-a-Coke bottle that was displayed in our home. The original bottle was part of a set Eileen had given me for my forty-second birthday. When I unwrapped the heavy rectangular box, I screamed with excitement. It wasn't the cost of the gift that delighted me; it was the fact that she had listened to me.

It was a pack of personalized Share-a-Coke bottles. "You'll never find one with my name on it. When I was a kid, there were never personalized things with our names," I had said to Eileen months before my birthday. Somehow everything goes back to my childhood in some way. Every time we went on vacation to Ocean City or Virginia Beach, I'd look through the personalized trinkets in the beachside gift shops. All the refrigerator magnets and bead bracelets bore names like Jennifer and Melissa and Samantha, and although I knew I would never find one that said Paria,

I kept looking — as if I needed anything to remind me that I was an outsider.

I pulled out each bottle from the box. They were printed with our names: Paria, Babak, Armon, Shayda, and Aydin. I displayed the bottles in the see-through glass shelves in our bar, among the crystal Waterford wineglasses and champagne flutes from our wedding, these bottles with the names of my little Iranian-American family being more valuable than the Waterford to me. I knew it was coming when Ava told me, "You're going to have to take that bottle down someday. Just like you're going to have to take down all the old pictures from the family room wall. One day, I'll have friends over who won't even know about the old me."

I ordered a new Share-a-Coke bottle with the name Ava, but I felt like it wasn't even a bottle with a name that you have to special order. Babak and I had spent months debating her name when I was pregnant, each coming up with our own lists and finally compromising on Aydin. Although that was a compromise, once she was born and we called her Aydin, it was perfect, and we loved it.

When the Ava bottle arrived, I took down the Aydin bottle and put it in the box the new bottle had come in. I put the Ava bottle in the center of the other four bottles on the shelf and took a picture. Although she was upstairs and I was downstairs, I texted Ava the picture. She came running downstairs and gave me a big hug, then looked at the bottles. *It's not about you. It's about her. Look how happy you've made her. You can do this.* I held in my tears again. I took the old bottle and put it on a high shelf in my closet, next to an old pair of knee-high boots that I haven't worn in years, but which also haven't made it into the Goodwill pile, because what if I want to wear them one day? A few weeks later Ava saw the box. "Hey, why are you keeping this?" she demanded.

Babak jumped right in. "She can keep it. She's allowed to keep what she wants as long as it's not out for everyone to see. You don't get to decide everything." He knew how hard it had been for me, how much I still periodically struggled with Ava's name. I'm not a sentimental person.

Well, by that I mean I don't hold on to things. Ninety-five percent of my kids' artwork has been thrown away, including all the Mother's Day cards they made throughout the years, because it's not like it was their original idea — their teachers made them do it. I believe in keeping photographs and albums, but not holding on to clutter. This Coke bottle, I'm keeping. It was a really special gift from Eileen, and the truth is, Ava's past can't be erased, and neither can my memories. They won't be.

Then Babak's mom emailed us an article from the *Atlantic* about transgender kids. The essential message of the piece was that maybe we were too quick to treat gender dysphoria. It gave examples of people who later "detransition," going back to the gender identity they were assigned at birth. This piece left me devastated, heartbroken, and furious. My greatest nagging worry had been that one day Ava would change her mind, that we were doing the wrong thing. That was why I decided to hand over decision making to experts, her therapist and doctor. If there was a 2 to 3 percent chance that she would change her mind one day, I wanted to be able to say, "I took you to the best people in this field, I followed their advice."

I cried for several days after reading the article. There were so many articles out there saying we needed to listen to transgender kids, take their gender dysphoria seriously, and be proactive. Why did Babak's mom send me the one article that said we might be jumping the gun? I talked to Babak, gave myself a few days to collect myself, and then sent her a lengthy response, part of which read:

> This has been the hardest year of my life and don't think for a second that we are making any decisions lightly. Even if there is a 2–3% chance that she decides to detransition, it doesn't mean that we are not making the right decisions for her today based on the child we have in front of us and the expert advice we are getting from the best people in this field. Don't ever send me anything again that casts any shadow of a doubt on what we are doing. You're either one of the people who supported us through this process or you're not.

A few days went by, and I didn't hear anything from her. She called Babak just to chat, and he asked if she had checked her email. She hadn't; she doesn't check her email very often. He told her how much the article had upset me and reiterated everything I had said in my email. She sent me an apology, saying that the last thing she wanted to do was knowingly upset me.

I had been similarly upset when our friend Caleb had said that we shouldn't start hormones too early because teenagers change their minds. But he had said that casually, without knowing much about the issue or our situation. Babak's mom had sent a long article. When people try to give you well-meaning advice, they often don't realize what you have been through or how you might receive that information. I'm not sure Babak's mom had realized how difficult the previous year had been for me. Even if I was completely supportive and proud of my daughter, that didn't mean that as a mother, I wasn't going through the hardest experience of my life. After that incident, she got it.

Mother and daughter, July 2018.

I was glad I had stood up for myself and my family. I was grateful that Babak was just as unwavering in what we would tolerate or accept from anyone around us. Parents are often divided during their child's transition. We were always a team. This process strengthened our relationship as we supported each other through each step.

At the same time, our Transforming Family support group was discussing an article and videos about a diagnosis of "rapid onset gender dysphoria," or ROGD. Much like the false studies claiming a link between the measles, mumps, and rubella (MMR) vaccine and autism, this is a false and fabricated diagnosis meant to scare parents. The diagnosis was being applied to anyone presenting with gender dysphoria "later" in life — defined as after early childhood. The sources claimed that gender dysphoria in this age group is due to confusion and peer pressure and should not be treated in an affirming way. I replied in the group emails that this diagnosis was essentially made up, not valid, a scare tactic by a conservative group, and not endorsed by the American Academy of Pediatrics. It confirmed my belief that those of us who could go public with our stories should. The narrative of what being transgender is and the ways it presents had to be broadened.

At the end of June, I walked into an exam room to see a four-year-old patient I've been taking care of since birth. He was there with his dad, who mentioned some signs of gender dysphoria. The parents had been very supportive, buying him whatever "girl" toys and costumes he wanted and going with the flow, but then the child had said something to his parents that alarmed them, making them believe he might still be unhappy despite their allowing him to explore his gender expression.

It was the first time in fifteen years of being a pediatrician that a parent had told me directly about a young child's gender dysphoria. Because of my own experience over the past year, I felt qualified to provide the dad some specific guidance, and I later called the mom to go over what we had discussed and suggest some resources. There have probably been other cases of gender dysphoria among my patients, but I suspect the parents didn't allow the child to express their feelings and said something like "Dresses are not for boys," and so it got suppressed until later — either that or the parents just didn't bring it to my attention.

I'm sure that this kid's parents benefited from increased public and media discussion about a healthy attitude toward allowing children to explore their gender: that was probably at least partly why they were supporting the child and bringing up the issue with me. I felt hopeful for this child's future, whether this ended up being just a temporary exploration or the child turned out to be gender-nonconforming or transgender. And I felt grateful that I knew what to say to the parents, that I could suggest appropriate resources should the child start to experience more distress. I knew I would be seeing more patients like this child.

In July, we had a ten-day family trip planned to Paris and London that coincided with my forty-fifth birthday. A few days before leaving, I got a haircut, trimming off a good six to eight inches of hair. My long hair has always been a big part of my identity. It gives me a sense of comfort and security and makes me feel beautiful and feminine. I had written a piece about my hair and how it might be influencing Shayda and presented it at an *Expressing Motherhood* show. When I cut my hair, I wrote in my journal, "I'm going to make forty-five the year of knowing myself and letting go."

What exactly did that statement mean? At forty-five, I still worried about what people thought of me: *Am I good enough for this person? Did this person misinterpret my actions or words?* I knew it was time to just accept that I know who I am and what my intentions are, and that any misinterpretations other people had of me were not my problem. I wanted to let go of trying to prove myself good enough to be someone's friend. I wanted to stop investing in any relationship from which I wasn't getting an equitable return. I wanted to know my worth and be comfortable with myself. These were all goals I had been working on for a few years, but I wasn't quite there yet. This was going to be the year that I would get there — no second-guessing myself. No trying to prove my worth. Just being myself and valuing my true worth and letting go of any relationships in which I wasn't 100 percent valued. With that mindset, we headed for our family vacation.

I was a little worried about airport security. Ava's passport still said Aydin, male, and the picture was of a ten-year-old boy. Now that she was a teenager, looking more like a girl every day, would they question that passport? We took her school ID as a backup, although it wasn't a legal form of identification. I asked her if she wanted to wear jeans and a shirt for the flight, but she insisted on wearing her long brown skirt, which she said was really comfortable. At the first passport check at LAX, the TSA agent took our passports. She was an African American lady, a little heavyset, with short hair. She looked at each picture and then up at our faces and waved us through. She did not hesitate even a second longer when she got to Ava's picture and then looked at her. Afterward I realized I had been holding my breath. I exhaled. But then the body scanner beeped as Ava walked through, and she was taken to a little room for a private search and pat down. I stood outside the room, my heart racing. Another female security agent who was standing nearby looked at my face and said, "Don't worry, Mom, it's almost done."

Later we learned that each time a person walks through the machine, the guard hits a button identifying them as male or female. So if the guard hits the "female" button and the image shows a bulge in the groin region that doesn't correspond to the female anatomy, the machine beeps and triggers a secondary search. So as things are now, every trans woman who hasn't had genital reassignment surgery is going to get a pat down. This can be avoided only by signing up for TSA PreCheck. It happened every time we went through security on our trip. But at every single passport control checkpoint, in LA, Paris, and London, there was no issue. The agent would look at the passport picture showing a ten-year-old boy, look at Ava's face, and tell us to have a good time. It was like everyone had on their best poker face; every one of the passport control officers was completely unfazed.

My forty-fifth birthday was perfect. It started with a run along the Seine and past the Eiffel Tower. Babak went on the run with me, slowing his pace way down to match mine. A run outside never fails to give me a sense of peace and calm and a feeling that everything will be all right, making me feel like the only things I need are my health and my body and myself. A treadmill does not give me that feeling. The rest of the day was spent sightseeing and eating with the kids, having a glass of wine with each meal. The day ended with us riding the Métro in Paris together for the first time. I love riding the subway anywhere.

There was no cake or birthday candle, even though I'm one of those superstitious people who believes that everyone needs to make a wish and blow out a candle on their birthday. Paris is not like LA: I couldn't just run into a grocery store and buy a cupcake and a candle. And yet despite the lack of this essential birthday ritual, the day was perfect.

On the train from Paris to London the next day, I thought about how different this trip was from my last visit to Paris, about thirty years before. When I was sixteen, my parents sent me from Pittsburgh to Heidelberg, Germany, to stay with some cousins for most of the summer. A couple of my aunts came from Iran to meet us there, and we did some traveling, including a few days in Paris. It was the best summer of my teen years, but at that time, I'd found Parisians cold and rude. When I tried to speak to them in French (I was taking AP French in school, after all), they would stop me and speak in English, their English better than my French. On this trip, everyone was very friendly. Ava got a few stares, maybe a few more than she would have gotten in LA, but overall, the Parisians were welcoming and warm.

Our days in London were even better. I absolutely love London. I could live there. I ran, we explored, we ate, we watched some World Cup soccer games in pubs. I don't recall any second looks at our family in London.

Although it was exactly the vacation we needed, when we came home, I was also glad to be back. And I was definitely ready to keep moving forward.

Sitting jet-lagged at the dining room table early on the morning after our return, I flipped open my MacBook Air. The laptop had been a present to myself a few years earlier, when I had decided to start a blog. It houses everything I've written. I opened a new document and titled it "Allergic to Hugs," writing about Ava's presentation from the time she was in my womb to the present. The opening line came from something my older sister once wrote on my Facebook wall: "Give Aydin a hug and kiss from me for his birthday, although I know he's allergic to hugs." I wrote about how, despite wanting to be constantly held or latched onto me as a newborn, sometime in her grade-school years Ava seemed to develop an aversion to being held. She would squirm away when people wanted to hug or kiss her. Everyone was aware of her need for attention coupled with her shying away from physical touch. On Facebook I'd post a picture of myself kissing her cheek on her birthday and joke that her birthday was "the only time he'll indulge me with tackling him down for a picture." On one of my younger sister Parimah's visits to LA, she offered Ava five dollars in exchange for a hundred kisses. Parimah always had a soft spot for Ava, recognizing her sadness and not being exhausted, as I was, from the daily effort to meet her needs. I ended the piece by saying that once we started accepting Ava as a girl, her aversion to touch went away — she started giving the longest, tightest hugs. She was not allergic to hugs, but rather in the wrong body.

I submitted the piece to *Expressing Motherhood* for their show in November. My first piece, about my hair and Shayda, had been presented just a couple of months before Thailand. This piece was completely different. I was different, my family was different — everything was different, yet the same. When I heard back from the producer, Lindsay, that my piece had been accepted, I was nervous but excited. I would get to tell Ava's story. It would eventually be made into a podcast, so it would live on. I would be helping to get more trans people's stories out, and I felt certain there would be at least one person who would hear my story and find that something clicked for them, just as it had for me when I listened to Cybele's Moth story. And I was happy to be challenging myself, doing things that were different from my day-to-day life and job, connecting — feeding my soul.

CHAPTER 11

BACK *to* SCHOOL

I had vehemently told Ava she was not going to start her freshman year of high school as a girl, and now, on the first day of her sophomore year, I was relieved that the turmoil was over and Ava would be Ava in all her classes. It was August 13, 2018. Armon was starting his senior year and Shayda seventh grade. Before school let out for the summer, I had emailed Ava's counselor, letting her know that she would be coming back as Ava in the fall, although legally she would still be Aydin and male. Her counselor was very supportive and had told me to touch base with her again in August, before school started. She informed all of Ava's teachers that they were to call her Ava from day one and use female pronouns, although their class rosters would still list her as Aydin.

Over the past six months of sharing experiences at Transforming Family, I'd learned that many kids change schools when they transition, finishing one school year as one gender and starting the next in a new school, with a new name and gender, where people don't know them any differently. We never gave Ava the option of doing that, and she never asked for it. When Ava was starting first grade, we had moved to Beverly Hills because it has one of the best public school systems in Los Angeles. Finding an equally good high school would not be easy, and given

181

Ava's academic strength, we didn't want to take the risk. A part of me was also still testing her. The narrative in my head was still that she was going to have a hard life and would have to learn to navigate those hardships. Transitioning in a school where she had always been known as male seemed like one way to start.

A few days before school started, I got a phone call from Ava's upcoming honors English teacher, Julie Goler, who had also taught Armon. She called to tell me how touched she was that Ava was being supported by her parents, that she would be a fierce advocate for her, and that I should never hesitate to contact her if I had any concerns, whether or not they related to her class. She ended up being exactly what she promised, a fierce advocate. I was touched that she reached out to me before school started. She was the only one of Ava's teachers to do so.

Although I was excited about Ava's first day of school, I was also nervous and emotional. And as so often with any big step forward, I'd found myself taking a step back again. The day before, I had gone to a Transforming Family meeting, this time taking my sister Parastou, who was visiting from Cairo. I said in the meeting that letting go of the old name was the hardest part for me, harder than the gender change. I confessed that I still hadn't started the paperwork to change Ava's legal name and gender. I cried and said that I was making a promise to myself in front of them to start the process. I still didn't think of the name Ava as my child's name. When I met a new patient whose name was Ava, I didn't think, *Oh, that's my daughter's name, too.* If I met someone new with a daughter named Ava, five minutes would pass before I thought, *Oh, I didn't say that's my daughter's name, too.*

But I also knew that I needed to allow myself to grieve and to feel rather than to suppress my emotions. By this time I'd been through so many cycles of this process that I knew a step back just meant I was readying myself to take a step forward.

Despite my nervousness, I made sure to take a first-day-of-school picture of the three kids. In the picture, Shayda is in the middle, wearing jean shorts with her hair in a bun; Armon and Ava stand on either side of her in jeans, Ava with a crop top showing just a hint of midriff. I posted the picture online with this caption: "The last first day of school for Armon who starts his senior year, Ava starting 10th grade, Shayda starting 7th grade....I missed a lot of first day of school pics for some of those in-between years, but now that time seems to be racing, I'm getting nostalgic."

It was the first time I had publicly used the name Ava, having avoided using her name or pronouns in posts while we were in that in-between phase. When I posted pictures of us at the Pride Parade, I just referred to her as "our baby." By this point, no explanation for the name change was needed. I had slowly revealed her transition to everyone in photos over the last year. The comments from my friends did not mention the change in name:

"Time really does fly!!!"

"Good luck to all three of them!!"

"I can remember when you were pregnant with Armon...seems like yesterday!"

"SO grown up and beautiful!"

Once the kids were back in school, I changed my work schedule, working the same number of hours but spreading them over more days of the week, a change I had been trying to make for years. The new schedule was better both for me and for my patients. While we were at a friend's fiftieth birthday dinner, the topic of what we wanted to do with our lives came up, as it tends to do on such milestone birthdays. For years I had been expressing my frustration with the way the practice of pediatrics had changed. Because of poor insurance reimbursements, appointments are limited to fifteen minutes, and then we have to spend time recording everything on electronic charts. It is hard to do a thorough job and address all of a parent's concerns in fifteen minutes without making them feel rushed. I had said that when it got to the point that I was spending more of my time doing electronic charting than actually talking to families, then I was done.

At this dinner, Babak said for the first time, "I'd be fine with you quitting your job and pursuing whatever your passion is, even if you made no money doing it." *What?* I had him repeat the statement and video-taped him saying it to keep on my phone. And then he said I would never do it, because I was the one who was holding myself back from what I really wanted to do, not him.

I came home and thought about it. If I could do anything I wanted, what would it be? Would it be full-time writing? Would it be going back into training to take care of trans kids? I've always wanted to support other women and particularly mothers in some way, which is essentially what you do as a pediatrician. Would I find some other way of doing it?

The truth is, I never consciously made a decision to become a doctor. I always just felt the expectation to become one. As a child of immigrant parents who gave up everything to provide their children with a better life, I felt the pressure to get the most advanced degree possible. But for Iranian immigrants, and I suspect for many other cultures, that doesn't mean getting a PhD in whatever field sparks joy for you; it means choosing a profession with a clear path to job security and financial stability. Majoring in philosophy or literature was not an option I ever explored.

I never really thought about what my passion would be. My older sister is an extremely talented writer and has a passion for politics and human rights. She got a liberal arts degree and then went to law school, eventually working in human rights and with refugees. I was better in science and math, so I majored in biology and then went to medical school. I never explored interesting electives to see if I might have some other true passion.

Though I never felt I chose to become a doctor, once in medical school, I was certain about my choice to become a pediatrician. I had always felt a passion for connecting with other women and for children. I once wrote a letter to Barbara Walters of *The View*, saying that I would like to be a guest cohost of the show for a day. I wanted to sit with women of different ages and backgrounds and discuss current topics. I started a book club with other moms while I was in Indianapolis and again when I moved to Los Angeles, thriving on the company of other women, discussing our thoughts on literature old and new. I briefly considered becoming a psychiatrist and also considered anesthesiology. Although anesthesiologists had to make complex decisions and calculations about medications, I loved their role in calming, soothing, and reassuring patients going into surgery. Pediatricians have a similar role: they reassure parents. When I told my mom I was going to specialize in pediatrics, her response was not enthusiastic, to say the least. "Pediatricians are woken up with phone calls all night, make the least money, and get the least respect among physicians."

"I don't care about any of that, Mom, it's the only field I can be happy in." I had known it within the first three days of my pediatrics rotation. Looking around at the attending physicians and supervisors, I knew that these were the people I wanted as my future colleagues. And the adorable and highly inquisitive and intuitive children were definitely who I wanted as my patients.

While I have loved being a pediatrician, I've been frustrated by the way my time with patients has been constrained by short appointment times and record keeping. Ava's first appointment with Dr. Carlson had been one hour long. I would love to spend that much time with each of my patients.

At the same time, I had been fighting our health insurance company to try to get the histrelin testosterone-blocking implant authorized for Ava. I had been working with Dr. Carlson's office, my own office staff (who also worked with Ava's pediatrician), the specialty pharmacy, and the insurance company for three months. The cost if we paid out of pocket would be almost $6,000, but Dr. Carlson's office staff told me that it should be covered by insurance, minus any copayments. I spent several hours a week for a couple of months on hold and talking to various people on the phone before I finally got it authorized.

This was the first time that I had been on the other side, as a parent trying to obtain coverage for medical treatment from a recalcitrant insurance company. Did I really want to have to deal with this kind of administrative work as a professional if I went into trans care? On the other hand, wouldn't I be an ideal person to do it, having experienced the frustration from both sides? Wouldn't I be able to help other parents navigate this complicated process?

While I was handling all these issues, running still kept me grounded. One day on a run with my friend Amy, I mentioned that I would love to take a writing class. Amy and I had met a few years back when we were both raising money through running for a charity called Every Mother Counts, which works to improve maternity care around the world. Amy told me that a friend had taken some night classes through the UCLA extension program, and I decided to look into them.

I'd always thought that once Shayda was in college, I could go back to school and take some writing classes for fun. Now I questioned why I should wait six more years to do that. I didn't want to be looking forward to my kids all leaving home so that I could pursue my interests. I wanted to enjoy these last years of having them at home and try to pursue my passions at the same time. Running and writing were the two things that I felt like I had actively chosen to do over the last few years.

I came home and researched the UCLA options. The creative non-fiction writing department offered a class called Memoir I that started on September 27 and met once a week, from 7 to 10 p.m. I usually fall asleep on the couch by 9 p.m. My heart racing, I signed up and paid for the class.

It was still the first week of school. When I walked into the house, Ava came running down the stairs to hand me the syllabus and handbook for the Madrigals choir. The syllabus had changed from the previous year, including the concert attire. Instead of "Men: white shirt, black pants, black tie" and "Women: black choir dress," the syllabus now said "Clothing option one: white shirt, black pants, black tie," and "Option two: black choir dress." Now anyone could choose either option, whether they were a boy or a girl or nonbinary. The choir teacher had also changed the official name of the men's choir to bass choir and the women's choir to treble choir. We knew that these accommodations had been made because of Ava, so that at concerts she could sing a piece with the bass choir. I was proud that her openness and bravery had led to these changes, and she was proud, too. We knew that she had helped pave the way for the next gender-nonconforming kid who joined the choir.

I emailed the choir teacher, Ms. Kim, to thank her for making the changes and also to say that I was happy Ava was paving the way for the next gender-nonconforming kid. She didn't respond; I'm not sure why. There had been some unspoken tension between us over the past year, starting with when I had emailed her early in ninth grade about why Ava needed to change her hair color for the concert. In ninth grade, Ava's hair still had a pink tinge to it, but Ms. Kim had said that everyone must have a "natural" hair color for the concerts. I had argued that high school students should be allowed to express themselves, and coloring her hair for a concert and then coloring it back would cause unnecessary damage to Ava's hair. She had just reiterated that I had signed the choir agreement, which stated that hair color should be natural. She generally didn't seem as supportive and understanding as I thought she should be. She was having her students sing a song with the lyrics "Love is love" for the concert, but I didn't get the sense that she was happy about having to make these accommodations.

While the change in the syllabus seemed like a giant step forward, almost simultaneously we also experienced a step back. A few weeks after school started, the Madrigals choir went on a weekend retreat to Idyllwild, a camping and hiking area a couple of hours from LA. Ava did not know whether she would be allowed to room with the girls, so I told her to email Ms. Kim to ask. Ms. Kim responded that they could meet a few days later to talk about it. At their meeting, Ms. Kim said that the school had decided that it would be easiest if Ava was given a room by herself. The girls would all be in one cabin, the boys in another, and Ava in one by herself. No one had ever asked me if that would be okay. By now the field trip was a week away, and Ava didn't want me to get involved in changing the arrangements. At the same time, she wanted to room with the girls; at the end of each night's activities, she didn't want to have to go to a room by herself while the others hung out together and bonded.

In essence, the school was saying, "You're not a boy or a girl. You are going to be put in this room by yourself because we don't know where you belong." How would that make anyone feel?

I was determined that this would be the last time she was singled out. For the next choir trips, I would speak up for her way in advance and make sure that we were involved in the rooming arrangements. And I knew it was time to get the ball rolling on a legal name and gender change so that I would have more leverage when I had to stand up for her rights.

In the end, Ava had a great time on the trip. From the pictures she posted on Instagram, it was clear that all the kids in the Madrigals embraced her and had no issues with who she was. I'm sure the other girls would have had no issues in rooming with her. I'm less sure about their parents.

I couldn't wait to see her at that next choir concert, standing in her long black dress and singing out in her beautiful bass voice. I was amazed that she did not try to change her singing voice to a more feminine voice. The choir teacher had once suggested she join the advanced girls' choir, the Minisingers, and sing in her treble voice, but Ava said that she didn't want to have to always sing in that voice. She wanted the option of singing in the full range of her voice. Her self-assuredness and sense of self amazed me.

I thought back to her first therapist, Hope, whose deep voice had made me suspect she was trans the first time we spoke on the phone. Once I had met her, I'd thought that Hope was lovely and I'd be happy to have her as a friend, but not as my adult daughter. I realized how much I had evolved since then. Now I felt proud and honored and privileged that Ava would be my adult daughter, whether or not the day ever came when she could always "pass."

Thinking back on that, I felt ashamed that I'd stopped taking Ava to see Hope because I wasn't comfortable with her. Hope didn't try to push any "trans agenda" on my child; she tried to keep Ava safe. She heard Ava out. She provided Ava with ways to explore her gender that would reduce her body dysphoria and depression and keep her from harming herself. And I had made the mistake of taking away my child from the therapist who was giving her exactly what she needed at that time. I sent Hope a text:

> Hi Hope. I hope you don't mind me texting you out of the blue, but I often think about you and just wanted to reach out. You were the first therapist we took our child (formerly Aydin; now Ava) to at Colors about a year ago. At that time, it was all so out of the blue and such a shock to us and I was just not ready for all of it. We are all much better now. Ava goes to CHLA for hormone treatment and has a therapist through the LA Gender Center. She is out to everyone and going to school as herself. I just wanted to reach out and let you know that she is well, and to thank you for being her first therapist. Paria

I did not hear back from Hope. I don't know if she ever saw the message. I don't know if she left Colors and her phone number changed, or if she saw the text and just decided to leave it alone. But I did know that I couldn't continue to beat myself up for all the things I had done wrong. I couldn't change the past; I could only hope to influence the future. I could share our story and hope that just one person might read it and handle the situation better when their child came out to them. I could hope that my story would have a domino effect, helping one person after another, until one day every trans child could feel free to tell their parents and be heard and supported immediately.

With school in session and Ava out to the world, she gave me the okay to share the short piece on scent that I had written for the *Washington*

Post. When I posted the article on Facebook and Instagram, the response was overwhelmingly positive and heartfelt. I knew when I wrote it that it should appeal to any parent. I felt its power again in the response I got. It confirmed what I'd figured out: I could write about this topic and get a broad audience, trans or not, to open their minds. I could expose people to experiences they might otherwise not know about, showing them that parents of all children, trans or not, face the same worries and concerns. All parents worry about their children. We all want love and acceptance for our children. We all have struggles with our children, times when we don't know the right answer and have to do the best we can with the knowledge we have. That same day, I started working on my next piece, about how having a transgender daughter helped me finally accept my own body issues. That piece was published in the *Huffington Post* and translated into several languages.

Through an email group for Transforming Family, I found out that the makeup store Sephora was giving free makeup classes for the transgender community. I signed Ava up for a two-hour class on a Sunday morning, and we went together. Three people came, and a makeup artist worked one-on-one with each of them. For two hours Ava learned all about skin care, and I finally learned how you're supposed to put eye shadow on.

When her face was fully made up, she looked beautiful. She was beaming the entire time because she was being treated like the beautiful girl that she was. At the end of the session, there was zero pressure to buy any of the products. We only bought one lipstick, since Ava was wearing much less makeup than before, mostly just using foundation. As her hair was growing out and she was looking more feminine, she didn't need makeup to make a statement that she was a girl.

On Shayda's twelfth birthday, I thought about how I had only six years left with a child at home, six years before my time would be my own again. But then I realized that I was already doing almost everything I wanted to do. I was running, I was writing, and I had my UCLA class coming up. I had improved my work schedule and was planning to attend the National Transgender Health Summit at UCSF to learn about the latest developments in trans care. I had pared down my friendships to the ones that mattered most.

The only thing I wasn't doing was traveling without the kids. It had been over a year since our trip to Thailand, and I had not felt comfortable going somewhere with Babak and leaving the kids behind. Except for one occasion, when we'd left them with his brother Roozbeh overnight while we went to Orange County for a triathlon, at least one of us had always been with them. I knew that I'd eventually have to let go of this fear of leaving them and plan a trip for the two of us, even if it was just for a few days.

In September, after months of wrangling with the insurance company, Ava got her testosterone blocker implant. We had a date at Children's Hospital to have the pediatric surgeon insert it in her upper arm. They would first use numbing cream, then inject the area with lidocaine, and then insert the implant. The whole procedure would take less than five minutes. Ava was pale and anxious, and I kept trying to reassure her. I had her drink water and take deep breaths. Again I worried about how she would ever handle gender reassignment surgery. I keep hoping that eventually she will decide she doesn't need it, that she is a woman as she is. And I keep having to tell myself that that decision is years away, and we'll cross that bridge when we come to it, just like we've dealt with everything else.

Every staff member at Children's Hospital was kind and supportive. The care Ava got for our simple five-minute procedure was nothing short of outstanding, and Ava realized that she had been anxious for no reason. Now that she had the blocker in, the estrogen she had been taking for a few months could start making a real difference.

In September, Ava got her new school ID. She immediately took a picture of it and texted it to me. Although she had not had a legal name change, the school had put the name Ava on the card. In her picture, she is wearing a jean jacket with a rainbow pride patch and several pins on it, including her "She" pin. Her hair is touching her shoulders, and her smile is genuine, her face radiant. The picture was further confirmation that it was time to do what I had been avoiding: start the process of changing her legal name and gender.

I drove to the Santa Monica courthouse on September 17, all the forms in hand. A caseworker at the Children's Hospital had done most of the paperwork for me, including obtaining a letter from Dr. Carlson stating that Ava was under his care and transgender. The clerk at the courthouse gave me a court date of October 26, 2018, at 8:30 a.m. I was shocked. I had been hoping it would take months to get a court date. "October 26th? That's in six weeks," I told her.

"If you can't make that date, I can give you a later one," she said. I thought about it. I needed to let go. We were on the fast train, but there really was no good or valid reason to slow down just for one passenger, me, when everyone else was on board and ready. It was time to say goodbye to the name Aydin.

On the same day I filed the papers, the American Academy of Pediatrics released their first transgender policy statement. It encouraged parents and clinicians to take a gender-affirming approach, stressing that they should support children and adolescents in the gender they identified with rather than the one consistent with sex assigned at birth, based on genitalia. I read through the whole statement, resentful that I'd had to learn everything in it on my own, but grateful that they were now attempting to provide guidance for pediatricians.

On September 27, I went to the first meeting of the Memoir I class at UCLA's night school. Jake, my yoga instructor and friend, had decided to take the class with me. He picked me up for class, and we took our own first-day-of-school picture by the front door of my house, right where I had taken the kids' first-day-of-school picture. I started the class with the intention of writing about myself. I wanted to write about my issues with identity and belonging, about using running and writing to change my life and come into my own, about motherhood and redefining myself after the age of forty. But within a few weeks, it became clear that the memoir I needed to write would be a blending of my story and Ava's. This was what my pen kept writing in our freewrite sessions, which our teacher called "mem-write" exercises. By the end of the ten-week session, I knew how I would start and end this story, and I knew that I would go on to take Memoir II and hone my writing.

On October 3, I got an email from the editor of the *Huffington Post*'s personal section. I had sent him my piece titled "I Battled My Body for 30 Years; Having a Transgender Daughter Changed Everything" just a few hours earlier. He wrote back, "Paria! Hello! And what an absolutely gorgeous piece you've sent my way. I'd love to publish this." My heart started doing somersaults. Over the past few years, I had sent several pieces to the *Huffington Post* about motherhood or identity and never heard back. I almost hadn't sent this one to them, thinking, *What's the point, they'll never publish something I write. . . . They haven't been interested in me before. . . . I shouldn't waste my time. I should try to get it published somewhere else.* The almost instant acceptance of this piece showed me that this was the topic I needed to write about. I was on the right path.

Other than Ava's name change, it seemed like there was only one thing I was reluctant to let go of. It was our old family pictures, taken on the beach six years earlier, displayed as large canvas prints on our family room walls. There is one picture with all of us, and then individual pictures of each of the kids. The photo of Ava is one of my favorite pictures of her. She is wearing a button-down shirt with light yellow and blue stripes, looking directly at the camera with the sweetest eyes, holding out a seashell. Her face is sweet and innocent, but there is a hint of sadness in it as well. In the family picture, where she is sitting next to Armon, she is all smiles, as she always is with Armon. I love all the pictures, but it was time to take new ones.

Ava on the beach in 2012,
Paria's favorite picture of Ava
that had to be removed from
the family room wall.
Photo by JD Murray.

Paria's favorite family picture from 2012 that had to be
removed from the family room wall. *Photo by JD Murray.*

Ava had mentioned to me several times over the last year that eventually I'd have to take down these pictures — that eventually there would be people coming to our house who had never seen what she looked like before and didn't know about her past. It would be strange for them to see pictures of a family with what appear to be two boys and a girl. I understood her concern, but to me she was still that person; that was still her as a child. These were my memories not just of her, but of our entire family. Then I thought back to her resistance at having pictures taken at her eighth-grade graduation and on her fourteenth birthday. I hadn't realized then that she wasn't just camera shy.

Those pictures were documenting her as someone she wasn't on the inside, cementing it as part of our family history. I didn't understand then how hard pictures were for her.

If I had to take these pictures down, I wanted to replace them with ones that I loved just as much. And I wanted pictures from Armon's last year at home with us. I booked a beach photo session with my friend Sanaz, who also happens to be one of LA's best wedding and family photographers. I sent her copies of our old family pictures, telling her that I wanted to go to the same beach, the same spot.

Family picture day started out badly. I didn't know what to wear, and nothing I tried on looked good. My old dresses clung to my hips, even though they were only a couple of years old and I weighed the same as I did when I'd bought them: my weight had shifted. I resolved to clean out my closet and get rid of everything that no longer worked, opening space for more of what did. I was done beating myself up over my body.

Before Ava got dressed, she came to my bathroom so I could help her. She was going to be wearing a spaghetti-strap dress, and so she wanted me to apply Nair to remove her arm and upper chest hair. She took her shirt off. It had been a couple of months since I'd seen her without a top. I noticed that her back seemed to have more hair than it used to. I felt bad, realizing she was going to be battling this body hair for the rest of her life. On the outside, her long hair and padded bra and feminine clothing made her present as female, but underneath it all, the story was different. Underneath was the wrong body that she was going to be fighting for the rest of her life. And I knew how exhausting it was to fight your body; I'd done it for thirty years. My fight against my body was just a fraction of what hers would always be.

I had spent my life trying to get my body to conform to some "naturally thin" white American ideal, but my body never betrayed my gender.

Seeing Ava's body, I again regressed to wondering, *What if we shouldn't be doing any of this? What if at the end of the day, she gets frustrated with everything she has to do to maintain an outside appearance that matches her gender identity and decides it's not worth it? What if we have to undo everything?* But even as I was having these thoughts, I realized how unhealthy and counterproductive they were. They were flat-out ridiculous. Plenty of cisgender Middle Eastern and other dark-haired women wage a lifelong battle against their body hair. So what? I decided to snap out of it, get myself dressed, and put myself in a good mood. I went to my closet and grabbed a dark purple top with ruffles and white jeans. I knew that white jeans would accentuate my curves, that the ruffle top would make me look bigger than I am, but I said a big "Fuck you" to the thoughts in my head. I walked out of my room and saw Ava in her dress. She looked beautiful.

Once we got to the beach, everything changed. Looking out at the ocean always grounds me, humbles me, and puts everything back in perspective. It is part of why "Sweat, Tears, Sea" is tattooed inside my left wrist. The photo shoot was fun, with Sanaz putting all of us at ease. It was nice to walk on the sand together as a family, Ava running ahead with the wind in her hair. She was excited to be getting her picture taken on the beach in a dress, and she thanked Sanaz for taking the pictures. When Sanaz gave me a sneak peek at some of the pictures, they made my heart leap. I realized that I would love these pictures as much as the old ones, if not more. We definitely looked older, and, well, Ava was the current version of Ava, but she was so happy. The two things I had been dreading, the name change and taking down our family pictures, were happening. I took a deep breath. It was all going to be okay.

Ava's new picture on the beach in 2018, to replace the old family room picture. *Photo by Sanaz Riggio.*

New family picture from 2018. *Photo by Sanaz Riggio.*

CHAPTER 12

IT'S LEGAL

I tiptoed down to the kitchen, relieved that the restless night of tossing and turning and trying to fall asleep was finally over. It was 6 a.m. on October 26, 2018. This is my favorite time of the day — the house still quiet, the aroma of coffee set to brew at 5:30 already filling the house. Six a.m. and just after a run are the times when I do my best writing. I poured coffee into the Van Gogh sunflowers mug that I've had for over twenty years — one that Babak gave me as a series of clues leading up to the ring he proposed with — running my thumb over the chip on the rim. I turned on my laptop, the glow from the screen providing just enough light in the predawn darkness, and wrote:

This morning, we go to Santa Monica court to legally change Ava's name and gender. It is a big day. I thought I would be more sad than I am feeling at this moment, but I'm not. It is an exciting day for my child, and I'm excited for her. And I have already done so much grieving of the past. I think that part of what is hard has been this feeling of not being able to really talk about her past, because she is still at the point that she does not want to. Memories are what keep a person alive. When someone dies, you sit around with people who loved them and knew them. You tell stories to each other and you keep that person alive. Ava hasn't died, but it feels like the old version of her has. It will help when she gets more comfortable with us talking and telling stories about the old her, because then it will be more like you're both actually just the same person; we just didn't know that you were not a boy and neither really did you.

Her new name, I've decided to change the narrative in my head about it. I need to stop saying that it feels like it isn't my daughter's name...it is my daughter's name...it is a beautiful name....I will develop an attachment to it. Her old name, I can think of as a childhood nickname that you outgrow...it's just not appropriate to call her that anymore. I miss speaking and hearing it and right now it feels like that old name is taboo to write or to say or to mention, but I know that in time, hopefully she'll be comfortable with me sometimes saying it...not calling her that either in private or public...but using it in context when it's appropriate...although I'm not sure what that situation is. I'm less sad about losing the gender today than I am about losing the old name.

In my memoir class at UCLA last night, one of my classmates, Eric, said that if he had to write his "six-word memoir," it would be "Lost son. Lost faith. Found self." When he said that, I got goosebumps. My breath caught. I don't know how many years it has been since his son died, but Eric seems at peace. Just the "found self" part implies that he does. I didn't lose a child. In the words of Cybele, I just lost a gender. But my child is physically here. I can hold her every day and I do. I can smell her every day, even if that smell changes a little or a lot from what it used to be. I can rub my face against her face and her neck and arm and feel her, even if that skin feels a little different now with the estrogen....None of my kids' skins feel like they did when they were newborns...people change either way...and I can hold her hand...I love holding people's *hands. I didn't lose a child, but I did lose a gender and a vision for this child that I had when she was growing up. But in life, things don't always go as planned. I can't plan every aspect of my life anymore. I can't control everything, and controlling everything is tiring and takes its toll anyway.*

I sat there reflecting on how happy Ava had been in the last few months now that she was out to everyone — being "out" simply meaning moving as herself through the world. I wondered if it was a little similar to the feeling I get when I leave my front door for a run, the sense of freedom I have from feeling the air touch my skin, recalling the years before I began running and felt like I couldn't breathe.

How long could I remain stuck in a state of grieving the son I'd thought I had, when I was seeing my child thriving as a girl? I thought about the new family pictures that Sanaz had just sent, and how radiant Ava looked in them. At the same time, I knew their arrival meant that I'd have to take down our old ones.

I would love to mix in these new family pictures with the old ones on the wall; that's what Babak wants us to do. Ava prefers that we take the old ones down. Maybe we will put up the new ones mixed in with the old and see if she changes her mind, although I certainly understand that in a few years, she will bring home new people to her parents' home who don't even know about an old her, and it will be nice for her to not have the old pictures up...we'll see.

The night before, I'd gotten an email from her English teacher, Julie Goler. She'd said that Ava was teaching her as much as she was teaching Ava, making her start reading more about transgender people and their rights, and that they would continue to learn from each other. I wrote:

I do know that I am beyond grateful for this child that has taught me so much in the last 17 months, just like she is teaching Julie Goler,...who will continue to teach me and the world so much. All my children are a gift. She is a gift. We are on this journey together...it is not just a journey of her transition but a journey of life...there never really was a true beginning...there will never be a true end.

I stopped typing and just sat in silence. What's losing a name when you're not losing the actual person? It's just a name. But it still felt like I was losing the entire time that we had invested in picking it out for her — the months during my pregnancy where Babak and I debated and kept trying to convince one another of our respective choices, making lists and comparing them, ranking the names from one to five. I also felt like I was losing the memory of how Shayda used to pronounce Ava's old name as a toddler, which we would still periodically bring up at family dinners: "Do you remember when you used to call him Ayeee-din? It was so cute how you said it." And now we were no longer allowed to bring it up. And maybe that was just the tiniest little thing to lose, but I didn't want to lose it. It was our family's tiny little thing. No other family has that same unique tiny little thing. Or maybe I was just using that memory as an emblem of all the things I didn't want to let go of.

I thought, *Maybe I need to just write and say the name Ava over and over. Like when I was a teenager and I wanted to marry John Taylor from Duran Duran, so I wrote the name Paria Taylor over and over and over in a notebook. Or when I had crushes on other boys and scribbled and doodled their names in my notebooks. Maybe I just need to keep writing Ava and saying Ava until I learn to love it as my child's name. It's not that I don't like the name Ava. I like the name. I like simple and pretty names. I just didn't spend months choosing it.*

All this last-minute chatter in my head was useless. I reminded myself that while everything else was changing, Ava's eyes never would. I could stare into them at any time and see that my baby was right there. I finished my coffee, put away my laptop, and went upstairs to get dressed for court.

I wore a simple black dress that would also be appropriate for work in the afternoon. Babak came down in jeans and a purple and gray plaid dress shirt. Ava wore her navy blue dress with polka dots, a nine-dollar Melrose thrift store find from an outing with her friend Enya. She paired it with the red saltwater sandals and black denim jacket I bought her from Zara. She looked beautiful, her dark brown hair now long enough to skim her shoulders, her big brown eyes shining. Armon and Shayda were not going to court with us but going to school as usual. It wasn't a big day for them. They had accepted their sister for months now, never slipping up on her name or pronouns.

Our appointment was for 8:30, but we arrived at eight because I'm always early for appointments. We got into a line of people waiting to go through security at the courthouse entrance. There was a chill in the air, goosebumps on my arms. Ava offered me her jacket, but I said I was okay. While we were standing in line, I couldn't blink back my tears anymore. They started to trickle down my face, and I kept trying to discreetly wipe them away. Ava hugged me. "Why are you upset, Mom?" I told her I was not sad or upset, just emotional. "Being emotional isn't a bad thing, right?" I asked her, smiling through tears. Over the last few months, anytime Ava became tearful, I would ask her if she was okay. She'd always reply, "I'm okay. I'm just emotional. That's a good thing. It means my hormones are working." She happily blamed her tears on estrogen.

Babak kept looking over at me, using his eyes to tell me to pull it together, and I did. We passed through security and up to the second floor to department K, room A203. It was my very first time in a courtroom — a first for all of us — but it looked exactly like courtrooms on TV. We were joined by others who were there for name changes, but we seemed to be the only ones with a trans child.

We were sitting in the front row, just a few feet away from the court registrar. He was a Hispanic guy who looked like a teddy bear, with a warm smile and even warmer eyes. To confirm we were all in the right room, he asked if everyone was there for a name change. He called up various people to go over last-minute bits of paperwork. He looked over at Ava, shook his head, and joked, "I don't know…your background check," then smiled and said her documents were complete. A cameraman set up in the opposite corner from the registrar. The court stenographer walked in and took her place behind her computer. Finally, another woman came in and had us stand up and take an oath as a group before the judge came in.

The judge, a white man, walked in. He was probably in his sixties, but you could tell that he was also California fit, despite the black robe covering his body. He was well-kept, with an almost movie-star air about him. I could picture him surfing early in the mornings before coming to court.

He sat down and again confirmed that everyone was there for a name change. He explained that he would call everyone up one by one, go over their old name and new name, ask the reason for the change, ask if anyone had any objections, and then call the next person. And then he said, "Please, no one should object to anyone's name change."

First he called up a woman who looked to be in her twenties and was changing her last name. She was wearing leggings and athleisure wear, looking ready to go to Pilates right after court. I could picture her having an Instagram fitness account. She said she was changing her name for business and work purposes. Next a man came up with a suit and briefcase, saying something about his long foreign name and multiple spellings of it on different documents causing problems. The judge said, "Okay, we're going to solve all your problems today. Please don't anyone object." He was friendly, making little jokes.

An Asian woman walked up. "You want to change your name from Helen Wynn to Hong Wynn. Is that correct, and why?" She replied that the new name had been her original name before she immigrated. The judge said, "So Hong is your real name. Okay." I thought it was so moving that this woman, who looked to be in her seventies, had decided to go to the trouble of doing the paperwork to take back her old name. What had motivated her to finally reclaim her identity? Another woman, who looked to be in her forties and Russian, looking very Chanel chic, was giving herself the middle name Irene because she didn't have a middle name, and the American convention is to have one. I thought, wow, this is a lot of trouble to go through for the sake of convention. Is she just adding that as a middle name, or does she maybe already go by Irene and want it to be official?

America is a melting pot of different ethnicities, yet look at so many of us struggling to establish our identity.

Then the judge said, "Ava."

She was the only one whom he didn't call up by her old name. She went up to the bench by herself, and then the registrar motioned for us to join her. Babak and I went up and stood on either side of her, while I continually warned myself, *Don't cry, don't cry, don't cry. You don't want the judge to question this.*

"You want your name to be Ava, A-V-A," he said. "Is that right?"

"Yes," she answered.

"Done," he said and smiled. He didn't ask her a single question. He didn't mention her old name as he did for everyone else. He didn't use his "Please don't anyone object" joke. This was obviously not his first time doing a name change for someone going through a gender change, and he didn't want her to have to explain it in front of everyone when the reason was obvious. He probably knew that trans people do not like to hear their dead name or have it mentioned, and in just a few seconds, her birth name would be officially dead. We sat back down and he called up the next person. We waited through all the other name changes, and then we were done.

While we had been sitting in the courtroom before the judge came in, with Ava between Babak and me, I got tearful again. Babak again told me to get ahold of myself, and I did. I messaged my sisters saying where we were and what was happening. I was happy for Ava, but I couldn't help feeling a little sad. It seemed like the official beginning of a lifetime of taking medication and possibly facing discrimination and having to prove herself to be a woman.

I didn't want her to have to prove who she was for the rest of her life. Proving your worth is an exhausting thing. I've done it my whole life.

Babak sent me a text so that he wouldn't have to lean over Ava and whisper to me: "Who would've thought that 14 years and 11 months ago when we gave her name for the birth certificate that we'd be sitting here in a courtroom about to change it." Even if he was not tearful and he was telling me to pull it together, he was having the same emotional experience, feeling the significance of the day.

But I also thought, *How lucky are we that she was able to come to us as a teenager, and that we could do this together with her... that we were required to be with her for this name change, since she is a minor. Think of all the trans people whose parents do not support them and who have to wait until they are adults, then go to courtrooms and do this on their own. We are lucky that we get to stand by her side and be part of this process. We are lucky that she included us in this journey from the very beginning, and that although it took us a few months, we could join her on it. We could witness it as it happened step by step and not have her go away to college and surprise us with it. I would have hated for her to have to wait and do this all alone.*

Doing this alone would be heartbreaking. Everything that I had thought was heartbreaking about the preceding year actually was not. It was complicated and unexpected and not in my master plan for my family, but it was beautiful.

Over the last year, my mom had mentioned a couple of times that maybe it would be easier if Ava waited until college to come out to everyone and transition. High school is already such a difficult time, but in college, Ava would have an easier time finding an understanding tribe. I said, "I can't stop her, Mom. I can't have her hold it in for that long and risk her getting depressed and hurting herself. It would be like asking her to wait three more years to start living. She can't live as a boy. And I want her to have the chance to arrive at college as a woman — a fresh start with people who never knew her otherwise."

On a much smaller scale, I'd reinvented myself in time for college. I spent my last couple years of high school planning it and stepped onto campus the first day with confidence. People who met me during my college and medical school days couldn't imagine me as someone who had hidden for all her teen years. But I'd been carrying the old me like a miniature doll hidden in an inside pocket for thirty years, letting her in some way influence every single decision I made. Watching Ava be so much stronger and sure of herself than I ever was, I was hopeful that she wouldn't let her past have a leash on her future the way I had. And with Ava's transition over the past year, I'd finally been forced to take that miniature doll of hurt and insecurity out of my pocket and put her where she belonged, in a box in the attic.

Babak texted me again, "You should look around the courtroom and take in this experience as it's likely the last chapter of your future memoir." I knew that, but I was happy that he thought of it. It showed his support of me and of my need to share this story, despite being a very private person himself. I thought, *Ava understands it, he understands it, and they are the only people I need to understand this.* I had arrived at the place where I didn't need anyone else's approval.

The registrar walked us all down to the room where we could get as many certified copies of the name-change document as we needed. I went to the side to fill out the required form while Babak waited a few feet away with Ava. The registrar's eyes met mine, and he said, "You have a beautiful family." I nodded thank you, and he left. I felt that in my eyes he could see all the mixed feelings and emotions that were being held in. He was telling me it was going to be okay. And I thought, *It is so true.* I do have a beautiful family, and he wasn't even seeing all of us.

All I'd ever wanted when I was growing up was to create this perfect family, to have kids close in age who had each other to love and support them. Armon and Ava had been joined at the hip since Ava was born. I

Outside Santa Monica courthouse, just after Ava's legal name
and gender change, October 2018.

had worried that the relationship between them would change now that
they were no longer brothers, but nothing had. They could still be constantly found in each other's room, playing video games together, or ven-
turing to Westwood to the closest In-N-Out Burger. They were still each
other's number one advocate, each other's best friend. They had shown
me that it's not about brothers having brothers or sisters having sisters,
or the gendered relationship expectations that we impose on people. It
was about sibling relationships and human relationships, and they don't
depend on gender. Theirs had not changed at all. That was the beauty in
my family that the court registrar didn't even know about.

Ava's name was called, and we went to the window, which was staffed
by the same clerk I had spoken to when I filed the papers and requested
a court date. We asked for four certified copies of the legal name-change

court documents, paid $25.50 per copy, and left. Outside we took some family selfies in front of the Santa Monica courthouse sign, and a couple of pictures of Ava. I took a picture of the part of the paper that showed the name and gender change and sent it to my sisters, who, despite their physical distance, had traveled the entire journey with me.

We dropped Babak at home to get ready for work, and then Ava and I went to kitchen24 in West Hollywood for a celebratory brunch before I dropped her back at school and went to work myself. I had given her the option to skip the rest of the school day, but she wanted to get back in time for choir so that for "good news Friday," when each member of the Madrigals had an opportunity to share a highlight from the preceding week, she could share with the class that she was officially Ava and female. She ordered a shake and red velvet waffles. I ordered an omelet and hash browns and skipped a celebratory mimosa, since I'd be seeing patients an hour later.

Over brunch, Ava was the one who kept getting tearful, reaching out for my hand across the table, the weight of the emotions of the day finally catching up with her. She told me that in court, Babak had told her that although this was a big day for her for legal reasons, to him it was not. He told her that she was already Ava to him long before it became official.

We also talked about the fact that although right now she was very outspoken and wore her pride jacket and "She" pins, there might come a day when she might not want to be an activist and instead just want to live her life. She said that she thought about that sometimes. That at some point it would be nice to just be a regular woman in the world doing her thing and living her life — passing.

I've been deliberating about that a lot — whether she needs to be a trailblazer and an activist just because she is smarter than anyone else I know, and because she has the family support and strength to do so. Do these advantages give her an obligation to be out there giving back to the trans community?

I don't want her to feel the pressure to do extraordinary things just because she *is* extraordinary. I want her to experience the beauty and peace of an ordinary life.

Do we have an obligation to the world? Do we have an obligation to ourselves? Which is more important? Do we put ourselves out there, giving back and spreading awareness and making the way easier for others, at the cost of our own lives and peace? I know that the answer is not black and white. There can definitely be a balance between these things. There may be phases in our lives when we are activists and phases when we are not. I don't know what Ava will decide for her own future, and I don't know what I'll decide for mine or how I'll navigate it.

Over brunch, I told her I would always regret the few months it took us to start to believe her. I apologized for saying no when she first asked us to call her by a girl name and use female pronouns in private. I told her I would always regret those few months of a closed mind. She tried to mother me again, telling me it was all okay. We sat there crying, holding hands across the table, lips quivering, staring at each other in the eyes, sharing what each of us had experienced over the past year.

We talked about my book and why I needed to write it. I said there weren't enough stories out there about kids who don't know they are trans until puberty or later, and that was a big part of why we were slow to accept it when she told us. I wanted there to be more stories for other parents to hear, so that when another teen suddenly comes out to their parents, they've heard a story like that before, and they don't immediately dismiss their teen the way I had immediately dismissed her. She understood.

"I think that's a fantastic reason for you to write a book."

So here is that book — the story from the day we got the phone call in Thailand to the day of Ava's legal name and gender change. And here is where I end it. The rest of the story is Ava's story, which she may or may not tell someday. I've told my part because I know there is at least one person out there who needed to read it.

ACKNOWLEDGMENTS

Writing a book is the dream I didn't know I had, although I've spent a lifetime wanting to be seen for who I am — to be heard. Everyone who has ever read a word I've written has heard me. Thank you.

Georgia Hughes, you had the perfect combination of enthusiasm and consideration for my family's story, recognizing the value of what needed to be shared while respecting the parts that aren't mine to tell. I thank you and the entire team at New World Library for bringing our story to a wide audience.

My agent, Jill Marsal, you believed in this story being told through my voice and never asked me to compromise the way I wanted to tell it.

I am grateful to Shawna Kenney, my memoir teacher, for her unrelenting faith in me. She read my entire manuscript and helped me get it ready for publication. Anytime I mentioned the possibility of self-publishing or giving up on this book altogether, she insisted that I would find the right agent and right publisher and that she would be first in line at my book signing.

Juliet and Katie, you knew I could write before I did. I'm not sure that I would have ever started writing if Juliet hadn't asked me to. What a priceless gift you gave me.

My little village of friends who were on this journey with me from the start, lending me their ears anytime. You know who you are.

I don't know where I would be without my support group Transforming Family. As difficult as those first few meetings were, they were exactly what I needed to be able to see my future self in you and know that together we would dedicate our lives to advocating for our children.

To Ava's therapist and doctor (referred to in this book as Dr. Stern and Dr. Carlson), thank you for walking our family through this time and making the decisions seem so clear.

My sisters Parastou and Parimah, who walked through every step of this transition with me, both virtually and in person, and have loved Ava unconditionally from the day she was born.

I would not be here without my parents Parvin and Hassan, who, like many immigrant parents, have sacrificed their entire lives to give their three daughters the best of everything and now continue to do so for their grandchildren. Thank you also for resuming watching our teenagers while we escape for a few days at a time.

My three children, Armon, Ava, and Shayda. The three of you are my reason for being, my everything. My greatest accomplishment and joy will always be the privilege of being your mother.

To Babak, for encouraging me to cross so many bridges on my own, and holding my hand over the ones I am not brave enough to cross alone.

RESOURCES

National Center for Transgender Equality — https://transequality
.org: The National Center for Transgender Equality advocates to change
policies and to increase understanding and acceptance of transgender
people. Its projects include the Transgender Legal Services Network, a
resource to ensure that every transgender person has access to assistance
navigating the complicated name- and gender-change processes and
other legal issues.

TransFamilies — https://transfamilies.org: TransFamilies is a membership website for families with transgender, nonbinary, or gender-diverse
kids of any age. Its members, moderators, and administrators are primar-
ily people who are raising or have raised a transgender child, are in a
relationship with a trans or nonbinary person, are trans themselves, or are
in some way related to a trans person. It offers a safe space where families
can find support and support other families navigating similar journeys.
Membership is free, and its online support groups allow anyone to join.

Transforming Family — www.transformingfamily.org: Transforming Family is the Los Angeles–based support group that I attended and

describe in the memoir. It provides a supportive environment in which children, adolescents, and their families can explore issues of gender identity. Meeting dates, times, and location information are kept private, but those living in the greater Los Angeles area can contact an administrator through the website to join the group and obtain meeting details.

Transgender Law Center — https://transgenderlawcenter.org: The Transgender Law Center works to change law, policy, and attitudes so that all people can live safely, authentically, and free from discrimination regardless of their gender identity and expression.

Trans Lifeline — www.translifeline.org: Trans Lifeline is a grassroots hotline and nonprofit organization offering direct emotional and financial support to trans people in crisis. The hotline is run by trans people for trans and gender-questioning callers of all ages. The organization is also launching a Family and Friends line to support the significant others, family, and friends of trans people.

TransYouth Family Allies (TYFA) — www.imatyfa.org: TYFA empowers children and families by partnering with educators, service providers, and communities to develop supportive environments in which gender may be expressed and respected.

WPATH (World Professional Association for Transgender Health) — www.wpath.org: WPATH is a nonprofit, interdisciplinary professional and educational organization devoted to transgender health. It promotes evidence-based care, education, research, advocacy, public policy, and respect in transgender health. It publishes the *Standards of Care,* which articulates a professional consensus about the psychiatric, psychological, medical, and surgical management of gender dysphoria and helps professionals understand the parameters within which they may offer assistance to those with these conditions.

ABOUT *the* AUTHOR

Paria Hassouri is a pediatrician, mother of three, trans rights activist, and runner. She graduated from the University of Pittsburgh School of Medicine in 1999 and completed her pediatric residency training at the Cleveland Clinic Foundation in 2002. Her personal essays have been published on multiple sites, including the *Washington Post*, the *Los Angeles Times*, and the *Huffington Post*. She has presented stories onstage through *Expressing Motherhood* and been interviewed for multiple podcasts. A proud Iranian-American, she spent her formative years in Pittsburgh, Pennsylvania. She currently resides and practices in Los Angeles, California. She can be reached through Twitter (@pariahassouri), Instagram (@laparia), and her website, PariaHassouri.com.